This page has been deliberately left blank

by the same author

It's Raining Cats and Dogs
An Autism Spectrum Guide to the Confusing World
of Idioms, Metaphors and Everyday Expressions
ISBN 978 1 84905 283 2
eISBN 978 0 85700 588 5

A Different Kettle of Fish
A Day in the Life of a Physics Student with Autism
ISBN 978 1 84905 532 1
eISBN 978 0 85700 956 2

WHAT HAS AUTISM EVER DONE FOR US?

How the autistic way of thinking revolutionised the world

Written by Michael Barton

First published in 2022
by Michael Barton

www.michaelbarton.org.uk

Copyright © 2022 Michael Barton

All rights reserved

No part of this book may be reproduced, or stored in a
retrieval system, or transmitted in any form or by any means,
electronic, mechanical, photocopying, recording, or
otherwise, without express written permission of the author.

ISBN-13: 978 0 95671 302 5
ISBN-10: 0 95671 302 5

"What would happen if the autism gene was eliminated from the gene pool?

You would have a bunch of people standing around in a cave, chatting and socializing and not getting anything done."

Temple Grandin, *The Way I See It: A Personal Look at Autism & Asperger's*

Acknowledgements

I would like to acknowledge my parents Andrew and Delia Barton for their encouragement and support assisting me with the research involved in producing this book and their help in compiling and condensing all the information, without which this book would not have been possible. Also, R P Moon for his enlightening insights, particularly with respect to Wittgenstein. I would also like to thank Kiera Greenwood for copy editing the text.

CONTENTS

Introduction

It was the year AD33, late afternoon, about teatime. The People's Front of Judea, a group of political activists in southern Palestine, were complaining about the oppressive Roman occupation and were discussing ways to overthrow them. The Romans had taken everything from them – from their fathers, and their fathers' fathers. "What have the Romans ever done for us?", their leader asked.

After a short pause, a voice piped up "The aqueduct?". Ah yes, the Romans had done one thing for the common person. But then the floodgates opened: "Sanitation"; "Education"; "The Roads"; "Wine". And so, they all agreed that the Romans had done nothing apart from the aqueduct, sanitation, medicine, education, wine, public order, irrigation, roads, the fresh-water system and public health. It turns out that the Romans had, in fact, transformed their society from lawless, disorganised poverty into a modern civilisation.

This is one of my favourite scenes in the Monty Python film *Life of Brian* and provides for me a wonderful allegory for the current misunderstandings about autism. Which is why I pose the question: What has autism ever done for us?

Throughout history, many of the world's greatest thinkers and innovators have displayed certain characteristics, or traits that are more common and intense in autistic people. Relentless curiosity, passionate special interests and the propensity for 'sticking at things', among others, being qualities that I suggest, are the ultimate catalysts for mankind's intellectual and technological development. In fact, I believe that it is because of their autistic traits that a number of brilliant individuals came up with completely new and radical ideas, which led to the world changing discoveries outlined in this book.

What would our past have looked like if we didn't have Newton's three laws of motion? His findings led to the invention of the steam engine and ultimately, the industrial revolution, a pivotal point in the development of the modern world. What would life be like now without Alan Turing's contribution to the invention of the modern-day computer? No internet or iPhones, that's for certain. What will be the consequences to the future of our planet if we don't listen to environmental activist Greta Thunberg? Her tireless work has brought conversations on climate change to the global stage and her unshakable determination has shown up many a politician.

Despite the autistic way of thinking being behind every technological innovation to date, most autism reporting is negative. Autism tends to be viewed only as a medical condition defined by the difficulties people experience. But, as an optimistic autistic person, I don't like being labelled by my weaknesses when I have many strengths. There is a lot more to autism than most people imagine and delving a little deeper into the condition proves to be just as enlightening as looking at what the Romans ever did for us.

I want to redress the balance and put forward a case to demonstrate that there are actually some amazing qualities and achievements that autism contributes to society. To do this, I have pinpointed a diverse selection of famous people, both past and present, to evaluate from an autistic point of view. The people I've chosen have all made revolutionary contributions to the world and I will explore the idea that their autistic traits were not just important, but fundamental to their achievements. This will highlight the contrast between the stigma of the medical model of autism and the immeasurable value of beneficial autistic traits.

I must emphasise that not all the characters in this book would have been diagnosed as autistic. An autism diagnosis is not based upon how many autistic traits someone displays, but on how adversely these traits affect their daily life. Someone like Bill Gates for example, might be labelled as a 'geek', but we could hardly say that it had an overall negative effect on his life. Others, such as Alan Turing, were definitely considered unusually eccentric, but fortunately their tremendous skills were recognised and they were thus able to make outstanding contributions.

Whilst I focus on the positive aspects of autism, I'm fully aware that we also need to address the negatives. Some autistic people may be non-verbal and require 24-hour care. This creates a conundrum: how does the same condition range from severe debilitation to Einstein? There is no simple answer, but we do know that autistic people exhibit a very uneven profile; we can be extremely deficient in some areas whilst being exceptionally capable in others. This is just one example of how complex autism is and how it manifests so differently depending on the individual.

If society in general were to be more tolerant and compassionate and schools and employers were to make adjustments to cater for autistic people's needs, then we could start to reap the benefits of positive autistic traits. As Einstein once said, "All that is valuable in human society depends upon the opportunity for development accorded the individual".[1] Some forward-thinking companies are already embracing autistic people. If this trend grows and the characters in this book are anything to go by, we can't begin to imagine what some of the extraordinary minds out there might come up with next. And perhaps most importantly, it would enable more autistic people to lead meaningful, purposeful and happy lives. This sounds like a 'win-win' situation to me.

In this book I want to achieve three things:

Firstly, I want to demonstrate the invaluable contribution autism has made to the development of our civilisation using the examples of a selection of famous people who clearly, in my mind, exhibit autistic traits. Being autistic myself, I am ideally qualified to analyse this aspect of their personalities, because I can recognise many of my own characteristics and experiences in them.

Secondly, I want to show that the requirement for autistic people's unique skills is growing more than ever in the modern technological age. Companies that embrace diversity and inclusion will gain competitive advantages from this skillset and will therefore be the ones that are the most likely to prosper.

Finally, I hope this book will help to change people's preconceptions of autism, from one based mainly on disability to one that also recognises and celebrates exceptional ability. There is a fantastic untapped resource of autistic people who could be contributing to society, but aren't being given the opportunity to do so.

So, apart from Einstein, Newton, Turing, Darwin, Mozart, Warhol, Gates... What has autism ever done for us?

You're about to find out.

Isaac Newton (1642-1727)

The concept of autism may not have been conceived until the 1940s, when Leo Kanner and Hans Asperger originally documented autism and Asperger's Syndrome respectively, but autistic people, regardless of whether or not they have been diagnosed, have been around for thousands of years. Autistic people are different to *ordinary* people, but as I see it, being autistic can be *extra-ordinary*. We have a different way of thinking and experiencing the world, which can make us appear to be a bit weird or geekish, but I suspect that mankind would never have progressed as far as it has done without our independent and divergent thought. It's both impossible and pointless to say that a historical character was definitely autistic, but being autistic myself, I am suitably equipped to recognise autistic traits and ways of thinking when I see them.

Isaac Newton is a prime example of someone who's way of thinking differed from the norm. This led him to come up with ideas which had a profound impact on how the world was perceived. It's an understatement to say he was way ahead of his time – he changed our fundamental understanding of the basic laws of nature. And, having had such a profound impact on modern society, there's no way of knowing where we would be today without him.

I studied Physics at university and Newton's work laid the very foundations of my course. When I look back, I realise that many of the students in the physics department, as well as the lecturers, had more autistic traits than the average person – certainly, at least, to a much higher degree than the rest of the population. The capacity to think very logically, strong attention to detail, ability to focus on a single complex task for long periods and an intense curiosity to find out how things work are traits that all physicists display and Newton had in abundance.

Why is he famous?

Isaac Newton is widely regarded as the most influential scientist of all time and the founder of modern science. He is primarily known for coming up with the idea of gravity – inspired by seeing an apple fall from a tree – and the three laws of motion, which form the basics of modern physics and mechanics.

However, without wishing to detract from Newton's outstanding achievements, I have to point out (us autistics are sticklers for accuracy), that this is a widely held misconception – Rene Descartes had proposed these ideas 43 years previously. Newton's novel contribution was to formulate the mathematical laws that governed the *forces* underlying gravity and motion.

Newton published two revolutionary books, *Principia* and *Opticks*, which are undoubtedly two of the most important works in the history of science.

Childhood

Isaac Newton was born on Christmas Day 1642, in Woolsthorpe, a small village in Lincolnshire, England. His father was an illiterate, but wealthy farmer who died two months before Isaac's birth. A short while later, when Isaac was three years old, his mother remarried and moved away, leaving him to be brought up by his grandmother. He spent his formative years in near-solitude, before his mother moved back home with his three siblings, following the death of his stepfather when Isaac was 11. Content being alone, he didn't develop a relationship with his siblings, preferring instead to keep himself to himself. Up until this point, he had received a basic education in local schools, but at the age of 12 he was sent to the King's School in Grantham, England.

Isaac was a lonely child at school and rather than mixing with his peers, spent his time reading and model making. His favourite book was *The Mysteries of Nature and Art* which was a manual for building mechanical contraptions and investigating the natural world. He was fascinated by anything to do with time and motion and would while away many an hour making model windmills and boats. One of his most impressive creations was a water clock, which stood four feet high with the dial at the top, cleverly driven by a piece of wood which alternately rose and fell according to the rhythmic dripping of water. Kites were another source of fascination for Isaac, who enjoyed experimenting with different shapes and designs.

During his time at King's School, he boarded in the attic of a pharmacist named William Clarke. Pharmacy work intrigued Isaac, who was particularly interested in Clarke's library and laboratory. This was his first introduction to what today would be called chemistry, but at the time was considered a subset of the controversial practice of alchemy.

He didn't do especially well at school – reports described him as 'idle' and 'inattentive' – so his mother returned him to Woolsthorpe in October 1659, with a view to running the family farm.[1] However, he had no talent or interest in managing an estate and was therefore entirely unsuited to follow this occupation. Despite his initial lack of success at The King's School, Isaac's strong interest in books, as well as all things mechanical, instilled a desire to pursue a career in academia within him. Fortunately, Henry Stokes, master at The King's School, recognised his potential and persuaded his mother to send him back to school. Motivated partly by a desire for revenge against a school bully, Isaac applied himself and became a first class student.

In June 1661, he was admitted to Trinity College, Cambridge, on the recommendation of his uncle Rev. William Ayscough, who had studied there. As soon as he arrived he totally absorbed himself in his studies. He was very insular, and rarely ventured out of the comfort of his rooms. All his waking hours – seven days a week, 18 hours a day – were spent indulging his relentless thirst for knowledge.

Cambridge at the time was a 'free thinking' university that encouraged its students to think independently and to read outside of the standard curriculum (which was based mainly on the work of Aristotle). Thus he was exposed to the new ideas of modern philosophers, such as Descartes, which sparked Newton's inquiring mind into thinking about the most pressing questions in science.

In a set of notes, which he entitled *Certain Philosophical Questions*, he listed the problems that he was trying to solve, including "matter, place, time, and motion...the cosmic order, then...light, colours, vision".[2]   He also wrote a comment indicative of his desire to determine the underlying principles of science: "Plato is my friend, Aristotle is my friend, but my best friend is *truth*".[3]

Adult Life

In 1665, Newton graduated from Cambridge University. Although he'd spent his years at Cambridge working on remarkable and innovative ideas, none of his peers or lecturers were aware of the extent of Newton's capabilities. He chose to keep his work to himself, sharing his thoughts only with the paper upon which he noted them. This may seem surprising – most people socialise and communicate

8

with their peers – but autistic people often don't feel the need to do so. Unless we are specifically asked, we don't readily volunteer information, so I can fully understand why he wouldn't share what were, after all, just ideas and drafts.

When an outbreak of the bubonic plague hit England (a disease that wiped out circa 25% of the population of London alone), the university was forced to close for two years and Newton was forced home to his family farm. Here, he continued to study, think and develop his ideas.

It was during this time, at the age of only 23 years old, that Newton famously said he was sitting in the garden when he observed an apple fall from a tree. This seemingly simple observation got him thinking about the *force* that pulled the apple to the ground and how far into the sky this force operated, and eventually inspired him to develop his law of universal gravitation.

It's a great story, but while Newton proved gravity mathematically, he did not actually invent the concept of gravity. Kepler's book *New Astronomy*, published in 1609, had suggested that planetary orbits could be explained by a single attractive force operating between the Sun and the planet, and Descartes had proposed that the fall of an object due to gravity and the orbit of a planet could be explained in the same terms. Newton did concede later that he stood "on ye shoulders of giants".[4]

Newton's novel contribution, and why he is considered the forefather of gravity, was the application of his outstanding mathematical skills to prove it all. He worked relentlessly on the calculations and eventually derived the formula that he said "allows me to explain the system of the world".[5]

Newton later described this time as the most intellectually productive period of his life and he wasn't joking. Formulating the maths of the force of gravity was only one of his insights, light and colour was another fascination of his. He had a small glass prism and was amazed at the way the prism seemed to cause white light to transform into a rainbow of colours – this was something that no one understood, or could explain at the time. Through meticulous observations and measurements, he was able to show that the prism was bending, or refracting, the sunlight, which then revealed its component colours. All modern optics, from lasers to fibre broadband, are built upon this discovery.

Newton's curiosity was boundless. As well as working on gravity, he also thought about other forces which cause objects to move e.g. an arrow in flight. How do you measure its changing speed and direction? No one had established how to calculate this until Newton applied himself and worked out three essential laws of motion, which are now taught to every physics student, namely:

1. A body at rest will remain at rest, and a body in motion will remain in motion, unless acted upon by an external force.

2. The force acting on an object is equal to the mass of that object times its acceleration – or, in mathematical notation, $F = ma$.

3. For every action, there is an equal and opposite reaction. As Newton himself described: "If you press a stone with your finger, the finger is also pressed by the stone".[6]

The original idea for his three 'Laws of Motion' came directly from Descartes' 'Laws of Nature'. However, the mathematics required to derive these laws simply did not exist at the time, so Newton had to invent an entirely new mathematical discipline. He called it his 'method of fluxions,' though eventually it came to be known as differential calculus. This was an absolutely phenomenal leap forward – it's impossible to imagine the development of modern mathematics, engineering and physics without calculus.

In 1667, Cambridge university reopened and Newton returned to study for his masters degree. A year later, he used his discoveries in optics to design and build a revolutionary new telescope using parabolic mirrors rather than glass lenses. It magnified objects by 30-40x and made the image much clearer, yet was 10 times smaller than other telescopes of the era. This new telescope helped Newton to make the first detailed observations of the moons of Jupiter (originally discovered by Galileo in 1610).

He was elected a Fellow of Trinity College and two years later the Lucasian Professor of Mathematics, considered to be the most prodigious academic position in the world (a post later taken by Paul Dirac and Stephen Hawking).

It wasn't until 1687, 20 years after first coming up with his laws, that Newton published his most famous work *Philosophiae Naturalis Principia Mathematica*, known simply as *Principia*. It was this great masterpiece that resulted in Newton becoming the most respected scientist in Europe.

Prior to publishing *Principia*, Newton had thought of attractive and repulsive forces only in association with alchemy, as micro-forces operating between the invisibly small particles. Alchemy at the time was based on the assumption that there are *hidden* connections between things, and as these connections were *invisible forces* they were considered magic, and thus alchemy was associated with 'demons' and condemned by the Church. Therefore, Newton kept his interest in alchemy very secret. Any suggestion that Newton was involved with alchemy would have ruined his reputation and career.

To understand this, it should be stressed that people's beliefs were very different in Newton's time; witches were still being executed and many still believed in werewolves and unicorns. But, Newton was a 'free thinker' and would not simply 'believe' anything he was told or taught. He took a rational viewpoint and therefore, was keen to explore all the available sources of knowledge before making his own logical conclusions. It was by keeping an open mind like this that Newton spotted a vital link between alchemy and the accepted natural philosophy of the time – the missing link connecting force with gravity.

Having retired as a Cambridge don, Newton took up the post as Master of the Mint in 1700 to oversee the recall of the old currency and the issue of a new, more reliable one. In the seventeenth century, the value of the metal in a coin was worth more than the face value of the coin itself resulting in one in every 10 coins being forged. Newton kept a detailed database of counterfeiters and was fastidious in arranging their prosecution. He held the post for 27 years, the rest of his life.

Newton was duly recognised for his life-time achievements. In 1703, he was elected President of the Royal Society and in 1704, he finally published his findings about the properties of light in his book *Opticks*. It was the first explanation of how light from the sun can form a rainbow when passing through glass or water – a phenomenon that natural philosophers (as scientists were then called) had been trying to explain for centuries. This was a hugely influential work, not just because of its revelations about the properties of light, but also because it became *the* standard reference book for experimental science methodology, i.e. how to conduct scientific experiments.

In 1705, he was knighted by the Queen and when he died aged 84, he was the first scientist to be honoured by being laid to rest at Westminster Abbey.

Autistic traits

Relentless curiosity
Newton was passionately curious to find out how everything works – how force and motion fit together, for example. He wanted to know what prevented the moon spinning out of orbit, and why an apple fell from a tree. Attempting to explain these phenomena was an extraordinarily ambitious and complex task, yet this is what he was able to achieve in just three sentences with his laws of motion, which are still used today to describe the movement of objects.

Unconstrained thinking
Newton was not content to simply accept what he had been taught. Most of his fellow students were happy to just follow the curriculum and learn primarily about the work of Aristotle, but Newton wanted to find things out for himself – his mind couldn't be constrained. He spent a great deal of time and effort researching other ancient and modern works including the 'taboo' topic of alchemy, which at the time was considered akin to sorcery. This freed him to consider problems from a completely different viewpoint compared to the stilted thinking of his contemporaries and in particular, allowed him to consider force (which others shunned due to its association with alchemy) to be a potentially legitimate concept for investigation.

Pattern seeking
Newton's unconstrained, free thinking allowed him to consider the whole set of available ideas without preconceived beliefs, but another essential trait that made his revelations possible was his ability to spot patterns and links between these ideas.

Previous ideas about the motion of objects suggested that different types of motion (e.g. an ox pulling a cart, the flight of an arrow, or the orbiting of the moon) all had different causes. Newton however, due to his pattern spotting ability, realised that all motion followed the same basic principles, which he outlined in his three laws of motion. This unification of all types of motion into a single concept, rather than separate areas for study, profoundly changed the approach to future scientific investigation. His work is often termed a 'synthesis' because the same simple mathematical laws governed terrestrial and celestial phenomena alike.

Logical thinking

Newton had an extraordinary capacity to think freely and find patterns, but there was one more element fundamental to his success: logic. He demonstrated a phenomenal logical thought capacity by expressing his new ideas through mathematics, which ultimately is the language of logic. Newton's maths skills were absolutely outstanding, as demonstrated by his invention of calculus.

Non-conformist

Newton wasn't one to do what everyone else did and had his own views about many issues. For instance, he was a devout Christian and wrote extensively on theology, but disagreed with the Anglican doctrine of the Trinity (that God was the Father, Son and Holy Spirit). He thought this was illogical and was unsupported by the Bible. However, at the time, any fellow of Cambridge, or Oxford, had to be an ordained priest in the Anglican Church. So, he was under pressure to take the holy orders and Newton considered giving up his position rather than be ordained. In 1675, he applied to the King for a special dispensation, and to everyone's amazement King Charles II granted that the Lucasian Professor from then on would be exempt from holy orders.

Attention to detail

Newton was extremely methodical and an accurate record keeper. This was an invaluable quality for conducting his scientific experiments, as well as overseeing the huge project of recalling Britain's currency.

Intense focus

At times he would forget to eat, sleep, or change his clothes, as he was so completely engrossed in his work. Even when he went for a walk in his garden, he would sometimes rush back to his room with a new idea and couldn't even wait to sit down before beginning to write it down.

A fabulous example of this focus occurred in 1696, when one of the outstanding mathematicians of the era, Daniel Bernoulli, published two mathematical puzzles and gave six months for them to be solved. Upon receiving them at 4pm one day, Newton worked right through to 4am the next morning until they were solved and proceeded to mail the solutions back to Bernoulli the very next day.

Tenacity

Any problem he encountered, he would persistently come back to until he came up with a new idea, or solution. He wouldn't give up; he would just keep on thinking about different ways to solve the problem, or answer the question.

He once said he solved problems by "continually thinking unto them".[7]

Social difficulties

He rarely considered other people's views and hated confrontation. However, his ideas were so revolutionary that they were not always well received and often attracted criticism. He was unable to handle any arguments, or heated debates, so would frequently withdraw into isolation and continue his work alone.

For example, when Newton volunteered a paper on light and colours early in 1672, Robert Hooke, one of the leaders of the Royal Society who considered himself the master in optics, wrote a condescending critique of the paper. This enraged Newton, who was unable to rationally deal with the criticism, and less than a year after submitting the paper began to cut his ties with the Society.

Newton was also engaged in another exchange on his theory of colours with a group of scientists in Liège. Their objections that his experiments were mistaken lashed him into a fury. The correspondence dragged on until with a final shriek of rage from Newton, apparently accompanied by a complete nervous breakdown, he almost totally withdrew from intellectual discussion for six years.

Newton was well aware that *Principia's* description of the forces of nature was controversial. Such a concept was heavily frowned upon at the time as being a magic, or occult idea. Newton neatly sidestepped controversy by claiming that he had no theory as to *why* gravity occurred, he simply provided the maths for *how* it worked. In his own words: "I have not as yet been able to deduce from phenomena the reason for these properties of gravity, and I do not feign hypotheses".[8]

Preferred solitude

Newton had little interest in human relationships and preferred his own company. This allowed him to be a workaholic without distractions from friends, family or peers and hence he was able to put intense mental effort into his work, which resulted in him making so many important discoveries in his lifetime. He positively thrived in lockdown during the plague pandemic, because it enabled him to concentrate on his work.

What has Isaac Newton done for us?

Newton unified the different concepts of force and motion, thereby providing us with some of the most fundamental laws of physics. He also invented calculus in order to prove these laws, which in itself led to major advancements in mathematics. As if that wasn't enough, he also discovered the composition of white light, which laid the foundation for modern optics, built the first practical reflecting telescope, calculated the moon's orbit to an accuracy of 10cm and made the first theoretical calculation of the speed of sound.

His first book, *Principia*, outlined the principles of physics and mathematics, and is the fundamental cornerstone from which the whole of the mathematical analysis approach to science subsequently developed. His second book, *Opticks*, was equally groundbreaking and became the blueprint for the experimental method of science, which is still seen as a defining feature of how we conduct scientific research today.

Newton's laws have been refined over the years (most famously by Einstein), yet they provided the principles that enabled man to go to the moon nearly 300 years after they were first published.

Wolfgang Amadeus Mozart (1756-1791)

Many people consider Wolfgang Mozart a genius, however, in my opinion, he's a perfect example of how thousands of hours of dedicated hard work will pay off. This exceptional commitment to a specific topic is one of the things that autism has done for us.

It was Mozart's obsessive interest in music that gave him the desire to do tens of thousands of hours of meaningful practice. Looking deeper into Mozart's story, it's clear to see that his creative work was a combination of talent, dogged persistence and hard work. Together with the mentoring and upbringing he received, Mozart was able to devote his whole life to his passion in music and rise to the very top of his profession.

Music has always been an important part of my life – not just as a personal passion, but also forming a key part of my social life. I come from a musical family and began piano lessons aged eight, practicing daily in my own time. There's no doubt that becoming proficient in an instrument opens up numerous doors in the social world and my musical capabilities have led to me being welcomed into many different musical circles.

Why is he famous?

Mozart was a prolific composer of classical music and many consider him to be the greatest composer of all time. He propelled the art to new heights. At the time, his music was considered very controversial because it incorporated lots of new, unconventional ideas and was thus perceived as novel, different and exciting. However, he had the ability to write music in all the different genres of his day and used his taste, talent and range of expression to precisely target his audiences, while still being universally praised.

His unique compositions are still performed and admired today as much as they were in his lifetime. In fact, he's probably just as famous now as he was then; so much so, that on 27 January 2006, all the church bells in Salzburg were rung simultaneously at the exact hour of his birth, in honour of his 250th birthday.

Childhood

Born in Austria in the midst of the Age of Enlightenment, a period of profound intellectual and cultural development across Western Europe, Mozart's contributions to the artistic world couldn't have come at a more impactful time. A child prodigy, Mozart displayed an exceptional gift for music from an incredibly young age and began his career when barely out of infanthood.

There was rarely a time when music didn't feature in his childhood home; his family were all musical people and as soon as Mozart's talents were recognised they were keenly nurtured, a support system that aided his early success. And, his genius was hard to miss. Able to listen to a piece of music and then replay it after only one hearing, Mozart's acute awareness of music was astonishing. He was so inextricably bound with the art, that he even learned to read music before he could write.

It was his father, Leopold, that took it upon himself to sit down and formally teach his naturally talented son, beginning piano lessons with Mozart when he was four years old. At an age when most children have an unbridled curiosity and are easily distracted by their boundless excitement, Mozart was quite clearly different. He was so focused and so absorbed in his lessons with his father, that he would lose himself completely in the music and the moment. His strong will to learn and engage in the lessons made his father quickly aware that young Wolfgang had a talent worth harnessing and an extraordinary passion for music itself.

But it wasn't just music that captured Mozart's attention. He had a general passion for knowledge that would engulf him completely. Anything that he was particularly interested in, he would devote his undivided attention to. Although highly creative (as his musical abilities prove), he was also extremely logical, enjoying the rationality of maths, puzzles and card tricks. To appease his restless energy, he was a busy child, always looking for activities to occupy his attention with.

Just a year after sitting down to learn the piano with his father, Mozart began composing his own music. Two years later, at only seven years old, he travelled with his family from their home in Salzburg to Munich for his very first public performance. They toured Europe with a successful young Wolfgang performing alongside his elder sister as musical prodigies in cities including Paris, The Hague, Zurich, Stuttgart and Brussels. The talented siblings were particularly welcomed in London, which was then the largest and wealthiest city in Europe at the time due to rapid advancements at the start of the industrial revolution. Within five days of arrival, Wolfgang was playing before the Royal family at Buckingham House (now Buckingham Palace).

They continued with European tours and between 1769 and 1773, he made numerous trips to Italy with his father where he performed at noble houses and gave concerts at every opportunity. The family immersed themselves in the music scene, meeting other musicians, attending concerts and listening to other people's work. When in Rome, Wolfgang heard the Sistine Choir perform Allegri's *Miserere* and due to his amazing ability to remember music, he famously proceeded to write out the whole score from memory, thereby producing the first ever copy of this closely guarded preserve of the Vatican.

During these tours, young Wolfgang wrote numerous operas, which were received with considerable enthusiasm. Like any proud parent, his father anticipated a professional appointment for his son, but when this didn't materialise, they returned to Salzburg.

Adult Life

Mozart soon gained employment as a musician at the court in his home city of Salzburg, but was unhappy working there. It didn't stretch him, or allow him to fully utilise his skills, so he swiftly left to travel Europe in pursuit of a better position. Having been lucky enough to experience the various joys of the continent's leading cities from an early age, he made the decision to settle in Vienna – *the* place to be for musicians and artists at the time – working as a freelance musician. It didn't take long for his career to take off; he arranged a run of successful concerts for the Viennese nobility, gave regular performances and soon established himself as the finest pianist in the city. Both novel and captivating, Mozart's compositions proved highly successful and his works were performed throughout German-speaking Europe, which firmly cemented his reputation.

Whilst living in Vienna, Mozart lodged with the musical Weber family and later married one of the daughters, Constanze, in 1782. The union was born from shared passions and the families were happily united; Constanze's three sisters, all of whom were trained singers, even performed in a number of premieres of Mozart's works.

Married life didn't take him away from his work and if anything Mozart's success continued to grow exponentially. It wasn't surprising that Mozart was known for his novel compositions; unlike his contemporaries, he realised the great potential of the newly invented 'fortepiano', which was rapidly usurping the harpsichord. This new piano allowed a much greater range in terms of volume and dynamics, as well as the ability to play single notes repeatedly very fast. Having a much more versatile instrument enabled Mozart to write music that could take on the orchestra on equal terms. Harnessing this potential, together with his creative brilliance, allowed Mozart to invent the modern piano concerto.

Although his obsession with music occupied most of his life, he still managed to make time to indulge in his other interests. From billiards and bowling, to charades, fencing and horseback riding, Mozart's passions were vast and varied. He also had a great love for animals, keeping dogs, cats and birds as pets. So infectious was music in his household that in 1784, even his pet starling learnt to sing a version of the opening bars of the third movement of his piano concerto No 17 in G, completed earlier that same year.

Mozart lived a short but staggeringly successful life, passing away aged 35 from a sudden illness. Ever restless, even on his deathbed, he was still working on his last piece *Requiem* – indulging in his passion to the very end.

Autistic traits

Incredible passion, persistence and determination

Mozart worked extremely long days (and often into the night), devoting the majority of his waking hours to music. As well as composing and performing his own work, he attended countless concerts and listened widely to other musicians. Although innately talented, his true genius was a result of extraordinary hard work, formidable determination and meticulous research. He described a set of six string quartets he composed in dedication to Joseph Haydn, as the "fruit of long and laborious effort".[1] He was happy to work long and hard, because he was so passionate about his 'special interest', the creation of new musical pieces.

Single-mindedness

His output in such a short life span was absolutely phenomenal. He composed more than 600 works, including 61 symphonies, 58 arias, 27 string quartets, 49 concertos, 22 stage and opera works, 26 violin and piano sonatas, 17 masses, 19 wind ensembles, 15 marches and 219 dances. Still working on his music up until the day that he died, Mozart's single-mindedness was unequivocal.

Followed a strict routine

In a letter to his sister written in 1782, Mozart outlines his daily routine, which always started at 6am even if he had been composing late into the night:

> At six o'clock in the morning I have my hair dressed, and have finished my toilet by seven o'clock. I write till nine. From nine to one I give lessons. I then dine, unless I am invited out, when dinner is usually at two o'clock ... I cannot begin to work before five or six o'clock in the evening, and I am often prevented doing so by some

concert; otherwise I write till nine o'clock. I then go to my dear Constanze ...

At half-past ten or eleven I go home ... Owing to the number of concerts, and also the uncertainty whether I may not be summoned to one place or another, I cannot rely on my evening writing, so it is my custom (especially when I come home early) to write for a time before going to bed. I often sit up writing till one, and rise again at six.
(2)

Attention to detail
His compositions were extremely accurate and precise. On the rare occasions that he made a mistake, he would attach a correction to the score. Even though he produced so many works in such a short timeframe, they were all careful, deliberate and polished.

As well as mastering the piano and violin, he became extremely proficient in all of the principal instruments, including percussion. This allowed him to get first-hand experience of the intricacies and possibilities of each individual instrument.

Not constrained by cultural convention
Mozart was bold with his decisions and eager to approach his compositions from new angles and with new ideas – he was keen to challenge long-established musical tradition and be a symbol of change. Two of his great operas, *Figaro* and *Don Giovanni*, utilised all the possible instruments available in the orchestra as an integral part of the piece, which transformed how operas would be composed in the future. In pre-Mozart operas, the focus was on the celebrity solo with the orchestra backing them.

Logical thinking/pattern seeking

Advanced music requires a similar skill set to advanced maths: the ability to logically interpret myriad patterns in order to make sense of the subject. Clearly, in Mozart's case, this logic and pattern seeking ability was highly developed. Maths and languages, such as Latin and English, also came easily to him.

Sensory issues

Mozart had a particular sensitivity to harsh, or discordant sounds; so much so that sudden, loud noises would make him faint. He also had a sensory craving for smooth, rolling objects and liked to handle the billiard balls, which he found aided his thinking and creativity. This is reminiscent of stimming (rocking, flapping hands or jigging a leg), which many autistic people find relaxing.

Perfect pitch

It is widely believed that perfect pitch is more prevalent in autistic people. Having this ability meant that Mozart didn't have to sit at the piano whilst composing, he could work out the whole composition clearly and vividly in his head.

Focus

His tremendous level of focus meant that he could switch from one activity to a completely different one instantaneously. For example, he would play a game of billiards and then in the break, focus on writing a string quartet. At other times, he became so absorbed that he would lose himself in his compositions and work non-stop until the early hours.

Perfectionism

Mozart refused to accept any standard short of perfection and so continually tried to find faults in his own work. He would play different variations of his compositions for hours on end, changing and varying each part many times and tirelessly going through every bit of the composition until he was satisfied. It's for this reason that his pieces sound as if every note and chord is in its perfect place.

What has Wolfgang Amadeus Mozart done for us?

His music has provided joy and happiness to millions of people. As with any great art, his music is interpreted a thousand different ways by a thousand different people. It's true genius however, is that it appeals on a personal level, as if it has been specifically written for the individual listener.

The invention of the modern piano enabled him to revolutionise keyboard playing and orchestral composition. As the pioneer of the then new piano, he composed hundreds of pieces, which are still played today by every pianist during their journey from beginner onwards.

He also transformed opera into a completely new theatrical and musical experience and his novel approach to musical composition provided fresh new ideas that have profoundly shaped classical music ever since. He has inspired countless musicians with his innovative and adventurous approaches to music, most notably Beethoven, and will continue to do so far into the future.

Charles Darwin (1809 - 1882)

The autistic brain is more detail oriented than most, thriving off identifying patterns. One way in which this is expressed by an autistic person, is to build up large collections of items and to keep them in a certain order. This helps us to make sense of the confusing world we live in and provides us with a sense of comfort and security, as well as a feeling of control. As a child, I had a variety of collections, including Pokémon cards, Lego bricks and 1/18 scale model sports cars. I was also obsessive about collecting data about subjects that interested me – I became a mini-expert on dinosaurs, sharks and astronomy, and would drive my parents mad on day trips by reeling off the full technical specifications of every single car we passed.

Charles Darwin was also an obsessive collector from an early age, accumulating a whole manner of 'treasures', from small animals and insects to minerals and fossils. Ultimately, it was this passion that led him to not only travel the world collecting and organising specimens, but to subsequently write one of the most influential books of all time.

In my day job as a data analyst, I examine huge data sets for patterns and then explore the underlying rationale for these patterns in order to reveal new insights. This is exactly how Charles Darwin worked. Rather than fit the data to support any pre-existing theories or agendas, he let the data tell their own story. This is, I would suggest, a typically autistic way of thinking.

Why is he famous?

Charles Darwin is probably one of *the* most influential figures in human history. His book *On the Origin of Species*, published in 1859, introduced the concept of evolution by natural selection to the world. Despite popular misconception, Darwin wasn't actually the first to propose the idea of evolution – similar theories had been discussed many years prior to Darwin, but none of them explained *how* evolution occurred. His novel idea was that the mechanism for evolution was natural selection driven by random mutations.

The implications of his theory caused great controversy for a number of reasons, two of which being particularly prominent:

1. It contradicted the creationist view that God created the world as it is, and
2. It also opposed the prevailing view that mankind was 'special' and therefore separate from the rest of the animal kingdom.

What set Darwin apart was the meticulously researched and exhaustive evidence-based science he published to support his theory. He knew that this was the only way he was going to convince people of his ideas.

Childhood

Darwin was born in Shrewsbury, Shropshire, in 1809 and was the fifth of six children. He was born into a wealthy family with good connections – his father was a doctor and his mother was from the successful Wedgwood pottery dynasty – and he was brought up in a freethinking, intellectual atmosphere, which most probably helped to shape his future endeavours. But, with his mother passing away when he was aged just eight and his father working long hours away from home, he was largely left to his own devices in his formative years.

He was a quiet, solitary child and from a young age developed a fascination with the natural world. When not seeking refuge in his favourite reading spot under the dining room table, he was wandering the English countryside on exploratory walks – observing nature and gathering keepsakes as he went. Before long, he had established a large collection of insects, moths, beetles, bird's eggs, shells, minerals and fossils. This childhood hobby would later become an obsessive, all-consuming passion.

When the time came for him to go to boarding school, aged nine, Darwin was restless. Most of the lessons bored him and he hated the style of teaching based on memorisation and repetition. The only subject he found interesting was chemistry, which he fondly recalled in later life: "This was the best part of my education at school, for it showed me practically the meaning of experimental science".[1] At the time, science was not considered a respectable subject amongst the officials of England's public schools – Darwin's headmaster made no secret of the fact that he disapproved of him focusing on chemistry over classics – and his love for the experimental subject led him to be equally unpopular amongst his classmates, who nicknamed him "Gas".[2]

His father was concerned about Darwin's performance at school, but nevertheless acquired a place for him at the University of Edinburgh Medical School, where both he and Darwin's grandfather had trained to become doctors. Despite best efforts, it soon became apparent that Darwin wasn't destined to be a medic. He found observing surgical operations unbearable (anaesthetics were not yet available) and, as in school, found the lectures (or rather being 'lectured to') intolerably dull. As a result, he neglected his studies.

Darwin's underlying passion was still the natural world, so he joined the Plinian Society in Edinburgh, a student natural history group. It was here that Darwin flourished amongst a fellow group of 'freethinkers', many of whom were English nonconformists (Protestant Christians who separated from the Church of England), and were therefore barred from graduating at the Anglican universities of Oxford and Cambridge.

Some of the issues discussed by this freethinking group were highly controversial in both a social and religious capacity. Topics covered everything, from arguments denying intelligent design and animals sharing human mental capabilities, to the suggestion that the mind and consciousness were simply aspects of brain activity without the need for a 'soul'. Some talks were even officially censored. This was Darwin's first direct experience of just how deeply new scientific ideas could upset people simply by going against the grain.

He abandoned the medical course after only two years and went on to study at Christ's College, Cambridge, with a view to becoming a clergyman. In Darwin's day Christ's College was a quiet and relaxed institution, neither academically rigorous, nor religiously strict. This was ideal for Darwin, because it would give him plenty of time to pursue his growing interest in natural science and in particular his developing obsession with the study of entomology and specialisation in beetles.

Adult Life
Shortly after graduation, Darwin was put forward as a suitable naturalist and gentleman companion on a surveying trip to Tierra del Fuego, South America, on board HMS Beagle. Darwin's father was not in favour of him taking up the position, but he was persuaded by

Darwin's uncle, who saw it as an unrivalled opportunity for Darwin to call upon his 'enlarged curiosity' and make scientific observations, as well as collect specimens and travel through areas then little-known to European naturalists.

So in 1831, at the age of 22, Darwin embarked on a five-year survey expedition circumnavigating the globe, which he later described as being "by far the most important event in my life and which has determined my whole career".[3]

During the trip, he observed and recorded information on geology and natural history, as well as collecting specimens of insects, plants, small vertebrates, birds, spiders, corals, molluscs, other invertebrates and fossils. Despite suffering from extreme sea sickness, he did this with enormous enthusiasm and commitment; in just one day alone in Rio de Janeiro, he collected a total of 68 different species of beetle.

Darwin was particularly intrigued by the variations he observed in the closely related species of finch he found on isolated islands in the Galapagos – specifically their different shaped beaks. It occurred to him that these changes arose because the finches had *adapted* to the varying food sources available to them. The fossils he found were equally fascinating. He noted that despite dating back millions of years, they still resembled the skeletons of modern animals living nearby, inferring they were related. He was already starting to form the links in his mind between past and present life forms.

Before embarking on what was to become a life-changing voyage, Darwin had expected to return to a future life as a clergyman, but once the expedition was complete, he was determined to dedicate his life to science – which wasn't surprising when the specimens he had collected, plus his reporting of the voyage, made him something of a scientific celebrity in England. Upon his return, he began to catalogue his findings and review his copious notes and sketches, with a new found focus: How are new species formed?

Committed to finding an answer, he began to formulate his idea of evolution by natural selection in which he proposed that organisms that have characteristics best suited to their environment are more likely to survive and pass their traits on to their offspring. He initially described this process as 'descent with modification'.

However, the fact that this process suggested that evolution occurred *without* Divine intervention posed a stumbling block. Darwin knew this idea would be contentious and he had good reason to be worried. At Edinburgh, he had witnessed censorship at play and previous theories of evolution (Lamarck et al) were abominated by religious leaders as heresy that would "corrupt mankind and destroy the spiritual safeguards of the social order".[4] He realised he was going to have to be extremely cautious and diplomatic about publishing his work. After all, his reputation and social standing, which was considerable by now, could easily be ruined.

When he married his cousin, Emma Wedgwood, in 1839, he rashly confided his thoughts on evolution, evidently shocking her. Emma's reaction confirmed that he must not make his views public until he had indisputable evidence to back them up. In 1842, Darwin, increasingly shunning society, moved the family to the isolated village of Downe, Kent, a place that he described as the "extreme edge of the world".[5] Fearing prying eyes, he even lowered the road outside his house.

Darwin spent over 20 years developing his theory, pulling all the evidence together and continually collecting data to support it. He knew his ideas were going to be provocative and therefore he wanted to be absolutely certain of his facts before publishing. In April 1856, Darwin began writing a three volume book, tentatively called *Natural*

Selection, which was designed to support his ideas with a deluge of facts. He was finally spurred into action when another naturalist, Arthur Wallace, wrote to him with a strikingly similar idea. Keen to validate his own ideas, Darwin condensed his work into a single volume *The Origin of Species by Means of Natural Selection*, which was first published in 1859. The book sold out its first run of 1250 copies within two days and it has never been out of print since.

Darwin's theory showed that all living things had evolved over millions of years from single cells into the complicated life forms we see today. He saw the history of life as a vast family tree with life beginning at the base of the tree. As time went by, different life forms evolved, split off and multiplied along the branches with every species represented by a twig at the end of a branch. He didn't specifically mention humans in his book, but confined his account of evolution to animals and plants, thus avoiding the tricky issue of human origins. The implication was, of course, that humans are related to all the other species.

As Darwin predicted, the book was considered controversial, but it should be stressed that he did *not* want to attack religion – in fact, the book was quite conservative and actually referred to God a number of times. Darwin was content that God created the laws of nature and then allowed evolution to take its course.

Apart from the religious implications, the proposal his contemporaries found most difficult to accept was that his theory also applied to Man. For theologians and philosophers alike, Man was a creature above and apart from other living beings and many conventional thinkers of the time scoffed at the idea that humans could 'accidentally' descend from apes.

Fortunately, the majority of educated people, including churchmen, accepted his theory. In fact, just a year after its publication in 1860,

Frederick Temple, Head of Rugby School and later Archbishop of Canterbury, gave a sermon praising Darwin for showing how God moves by natural processes. On the other hand, Darwin was denied a knighthood for his achievements after Queen Victoria's ecclesiastical advisers objected.

Even today, more than 160 years after publication, Darwin's theory still causes great controversy and is still condemned by many religious people because it contradicts the biblical creation story and undermines claims about the literal truth of the Bible. For example, a 2017 Gallup creationism survey found that 38% of adults in the United States inclined to the belief that "God created humans in their present form at one time within the last 10,000 years".[6]

Darwin was ultimately honoured for his life's work when he was one of only five nineteenth-century non-royals to be given a state funeral. The accolade continued with his burial in Westminster Abbey, close to Isaac Newton. Today, he is celebrated as the pinnacle of scientific endeavour in the Natural History Museum, where his statue, carved in exquisite white marble, sits at the top of the stairs overlooking the atrium hall.

Autistic traits

Special interests
Darwin devoted his life to the study of organisms, including research into some incredibly specialised topics. One reason for the many years it took him to actually publish his theory of evolution was that he worried about being ridiculed by both the religious *and* scientific communities for proposing such a radical and outlandish theory. He therefore decided that the only way he would ever be taken seriously was if he became a world expert in a specific biological field.

He chose the study of barnacles, because there was no definitive work on them and the whole field of barnacle classification needed to be rewritten. This isn't quite as obscure a topic as it may seem at first glance; Britain was of course a seafaring nation and one of the biggest problems affecting the speed of the wooden ships of the time was the growth of barnacles on the hull. He specialised in this field for eight years, producing *the* authoritative account on the subject, which earned him the reputation as a world expert biologist.

In the latter stage of his life, he conducted an in-depth study of earthworms. He was fascinated by their behaviour and tested their intelligence, sensitivity to noise, light and sound and what food they ate. In fact, his last known work, published in 1881, was *The Formation of Vegetable Mould Through the Action of Worms*, in which he highlights the vital importance of the lowly earthworm. Such was Darwin's fame by then that the seemingly niche book sold thousands of copies in its first few weeks.

Compulsive collecting
Throughout his life, Darwin was obsessed with collecting specimens of the natural world. He relished cataloguing his collections in great detail and looking for patterns in the specimens' features. During the voyage of the Beagle, Darwin shipped home thousands of geological,

botanical and zoological specimens, to be studied and classified on his return.

Whilst studying in Cambridge, he built up an impressive collection of beetles and even had to order a special cabinet in which to house them in his student rooms. Over the years, he befriended many entomologists, visiting some in London who would give him specimens to add to his collection. He then wrote notes next to the descriptions of 281 species in Stephens' *Illustrations of British entomology*, recording when and where he collected a species, or the name of the person who had given him the specimen. Going out beetling was one of his favourite things to do and when 13 species of beetle he had collected were featured in a later edition of Stephens' book, Darwin was beside himself with joy, commenting "No poet ever felt more delight at seeing his first poem published".[7]

Curiosity

Darwin was bored by school and hated the rote learning method of traditional education. He preferred to think for himself rather than blindly accepting classic literature without questioning what he was taught. Most children at school strive to fit in with their social group and so conform without question. The autistic brain thinks differently and isn't as constrained by social pressures, tending instead to ask: 'Why are we doing it like this? What's the point in learning all this stuff?'

In other words, Darwin wasn't just a collector and finder of patterns, he was also obsessed about *why* these patterns occurred; a direct result of one of his other prominent autistic traits, intense curiosity. He had a burning desire to get to the very bottom of things – having to know not just *how*, but *why*.

Tenacity

Darwin is a perfect example of someone using their intense powers of concentration and determination to pursue their special interest and ultimately become the world's leading expert on a topic. Being financially independent meant he did not need to earn a living, so he could spend all his time on his studies. 20 years spent in deep thought before publishing *On the Origin of Species* required not just hyper-focus, but one other vital ingredient: tenacity. Even after publication, he spent a large percentage of his time over the next 12 years answering his critics and modifying the book, which became 25% longer as a result.

Pattern seeker

Darwin himself said, "I had a habit of energetic industry and concentrated attention to whatever I was engaged in. Everything about which I thought or read was made to bear directly on what I had seen and was likely to see; and this habit of mind was continued during the five years of the voyage".[8] In other words, he was constantly looking for links between ideas, trying to see if any patterns might emerge.

On his return from the voyage on HMS Beagle in 1836, Darwin set to work trying to solve the problem of the origin of all the diverse species of plants and animals in the world. Where did newly arrived species come from? He started by collecting the facts: "I worked without any theory, but just collected facts on a wholesale scale".[9]

Once he had a large enough set of facts he started to look for patterns, and it was as a result of reading an essay by Thomas Malthus that he suddenly spotted the link that provided his epiphany:

> In October 1838 I happened to read for amusement, Thomas Malthus' *Essay on the Principle of Population*, and

being well prepared to appreciate the struggle for existence which everywhere goes on and from long-continued observation of the habit of animals and plants, it at once struck me that under these circumstances favourable variations would tend to be preserved, and unfavourable ones to be destroyed. The result of this would be the formation of new species. Here, then, I had at last got a theory by which to work.[10]

Meticulous record keeper
The notes and records he kept during the five-year voyage around the world were all documented in great detail, thus providing the data for future analysis on his return. In all, he had about 1300 pages of notes on geology, around 370 pages on zoology, a catalogue of 1529 collected species, as well as 3907 other specimens.

Avoided difficult social situations
One reason he moved to Downe House in the Kent countryside was to get away from the stress of socialising in London. He preferred to converse with people mainly through letters, rather than meeting face to face, and he despised any form of confrontation. In fact, stressful interactions with people would quite literally make him sick.

Despite avoiding many social situations, he was perfectly happy when mixing with people with whom he had a common interest. For example, he loved being with pigeon fanciers, who were effectively practicing his theory in real life by breeding pigeons with desirable traits and selecting the best characteristics.

Free thinker
Darwin enjoyed being a member of the Plinian society at Edinburgh University, a group of free-thinking students who openly discussed radical, and often controversial, ideas with each other. Darwin's

thoughts about this were expressed in a letter to a friend: "there was a knot of men who were far from being the indifferent and dull listeners which you expect".[11]

Logical thinker

He used his logical approach not only in his scientific endeavours, but also in personal matters. For example, to aid his decision whether or not to get married, he compiled a list of pros and cons:

Marry	Not marry
• Children	• No children
• Constant companion and friend in old age	• No one to care for one in old age
• Object to be beloved and played with – better than a dog anyhow	• Freedom to go where one liked
• Home and someone to take care of house	• Conversation with clever men
• Charms of music and female chit-chat	• Not forced to visit relatives
• These things are good for one's health but a terrible loss of time	• Not to have the expense and anxiety of children
• Loss of time – cannot read in the evenings	
• Less money for books	

His conclusion was to marry.

Love of routine

He would follow a strict daily schedule and take long walks, walking the same route at midday every day along the 'thinking path' where he worked his ideas out in his mind. His schedule was:

07:45 - 08:00	Breakfast alone
08:00 - 09:30	Work in his study
09:30 - 10:30	Reading letters
10:30 - 12:00	Work
12:00 - 13:00	Walked around the garden
13:00 - 15:00	Lunch followed by reading the newspaper to keep up with politics.
15:00 - 16:00	A rest in his bedroom
16:00 - 16:30	Another short walk
16:30 - 17:30	Work in the study
17:30 - 18:00	Time in the drawing room
18:00 - 19:30	Dinner.

He spent the evenings playing backgammon with Emma listening to her playing the piano and reading scientific books.

22:30   Retire to bed

Attention to detail

It was Darwin's attention to detail that resulted in *The Origin of Species* withstanding the test of time. Darwin had a 'golden rule of counter-intuition', whereby he would pay special attention to anything which appeared to contradict his findings and work out a counter argument. He was therefore very well prepared whenever anyone questioned his work.

It's remarkable that his book has been in constant publication for over 160 years; even today scientists still widely accept his theory as being the best evidence-based explanation for the diversity of life on Earth and its origins. It is also a theory in the truest sense of the word: an interlocking and consistent system of empirical observations and testable hypotheses that has never failed scrutiny. Nothing has ever been discovered that falsifies any part of it, despite strenuous efforts by detractors.

Fair and honest

When he received a letter from Arthur Wallace describing an almost identical theory (the development of species through natural selection), Darwin was both dismayed and alarmed that Wallace might preempt his own work by announcing the theory before him. Ashamed of his "trumpery feelings" of disappointment that his "priority" of discovery was compromised, he recognised and respected Wallace's achievement, and being fair and honest, didn't want to take all the credit for the idea.[12] Hence Darwin's original manuscript, along with Wallace's, was read out at a meeting of the Linnean Society in London shortly before publication of his book. Wallace in turn was happy with the joint presentation, as he knew that Darwin had been working on his theory for many years and was honoured to have his work presented alongside Darwin's in front of a prestigious society.

What has Charles Darwin done for us?

On the Origin of Species transformed our understanding of the natural world and our place in it. The iconic work allowed scientific progress the freedom to blossom without being impeded by religious oversight, because it provided indisputable evidence that nature was governed by fundamental laws and basic principles.

His work also provided the fundamental building blocks on which the science of biology has progressed ever since. His observations about heredity paved the way for the field of genetics, the discovery of chromosomes and the structure of DNA, which explained the molecular workings of genetic variation.

Perhaps his true genius was the diplomacy with which he showed that God and science could happily co-exist. By proposing that God set the universe in motion and then stepped back, allowing it to unfold according to the Laws of Nature, he gained agreement from both sides. It then seems to me that, rather than the divisive figure he's sometimes portrayed as, he was actually more of a unifying force – hence his recognition in the two 'cathedrals of thought', Westminster Abbey and the Natural History Museum.

To that end, I see his greatest legacy as being the message that tolerance and respect for disagreement, along with meticulously researched evidence-based science, is the best way to advance the cause of knowledge. A wise man indeed.

Lewis Carroll (1832-1898)

Autistic people often appear to be very different from the norm and struggle to fit into a socially driven world. Lewis Carroll was most definitely different and biographers of Carroll describe him as a puzzle, an enigma, a complex human being defying comprehension. But, he was also a remarkable man with many talents and revealingly said of himself: "I'm not strange, weird, off, nor crazy. My reality is just different from yours".[1]

I can relate to this, because it reminds me of a question that I'm commonly asked during Q&A sessions after my talks: what's it like to be autistic? As far as I'm concerned, there is nothing strange, weird or crazy about me. I'm logical, tenacious, very honest and I have a good sense of humour (or so I'm told!). From my frame of reference, it's neurotypicals who exhibit strange behaviour – illogical, emotional, irrational etc. And by 'neurotypical', I mean any ordinary person who does not display autistic traits.

It's clear to me that society needs people who think differently. Diversity is an integral part of what makes us human; we're *all* on the human spectrum and we're *all* unique. As showcased in this book, different thoughts and alternative approaches have led to a flourishing culture and the development of modern-day civilisation. And apart from all that, wouldn't life be boring if everyone was the same?

Why is he famous?

Lewis Carroll was one of the greatest innovators in the field of children's literature and dramatically transformed the traditional way in which books were written for children. He was the author of *Alice's Adventures in Wonderland*, potentially *the* most famous children's book ever written, which is enjoyed by children and adults alike. It has been translated into 174 different languages, from Afrikaans to Zulu, and hasn't been out of print since it was first published in 1875. *Alice's Adventures in Wonderland* was followed by *Through the Looking-Glass* and together, these two books are said to be the most quoted texts after the Bible and Shakespeare. Nearly 150 years on, they are still so popular that their enchantment is celebrated with an annual event in Oxford called 'Alice's Day'.

A prolific writer and inventor of fantastical worlds, Carroll is also famous for his whimsical verse. *Jabberwocky*, with its wild characters, is considered by many to be one of the greatest nonsense poems ever written, whilst *The Hunting of the Snark*, is the longest nonsense poem in the English language and has even built up a dedicated Snark fan club.

But beyond writing, Carroll's talents were multi-faceted. One of his passions was photography, which was still a fairly new concept at the time – he was a pioneer of the art and became one of the finest portrait photographers of children in the nineteenth century.

Childhood

Born Charles Lutwidge Dodgson, Carroll was brought up in the remote village of Daresbury, Cheshire, where his father was a rector.

As one of 11 children, his childhood was busy and the household was always full of life, despite them having few friends outside of the family.

The Dodgson children were homeschooled and when not studying, would entertain themselves with plenty of puppet shows, mysteries and make-believe. Carroll's particular talent for inventing games, crafting stories and penning poetry was evident from early on and he would often come up with fantastical ways to amuse his brothers and sisters – particularly enjoying magic tricks. When not creating his own means of entertainment, he could be found with his nose in a book; reading was a great passion of Carroll's from a young age and was a form of escapism that he would often indulge in. In 1843, the family moved to Croft in Yorkshire, and it was here that he first started writing 'professionally' for the Rectory Magazine, aged just 12.

After what was a fairly whimsical childhood in the British countryside, Carroll entered the world of formal education as a young adolescent. But, after the freedom he'd experienced thus far in life and having only ever *really* socialised with his siblings, he thoroughly disliked his time at school. Bullying was rife and Charles was often a target due to his innate shyness and tendency to stammer. The lessons weren't much better; he hated the fact that he was expected to learn topics without explanation, instead wanting a full and logical understanding of them. In the words of his headmaster "he will not rest satisfied without a most exact solution of whatever appears to him obscure".[2] Despite such struggles, he excelled at his schoolwork and in 1850 went on to Oxford University to study mathematics.

Adult Life
Carroll lived his entire adult life at Christ Church, Oxford's largest college, first as a student and then as a lecturer. Described as a

modest, unassuming man he was tall and slender with unfashionably long wavy brown hair. Ordained in 1861, he became The Reverend Dodgson, and always wore black clergyman's clothes in the college. He had a very formal manner – proper in every detail of behaviour – yet beneath this severe exterior was a funny and insightful man, with a soaring imagination.

Over the years, he became a highly respected Professor of Mathematics and Logic, writing 11 books on the subject. His work covered topics such as linear algebra, geometry and logic, and broke new ground in many areas. Even today, his work is regularly referred to in scientific journals and some of his papers have recently had a resurgence in current areas of mathematical research, such as matrix theory and combinatorial mathematics. However, his great love of poetry and story writing (which he is famed for) was what he pursued in his spare time with enormous passion.

Carroll was close friends with the Dean of the college, who had four children. He enjoyed their company immensely and took great pleasure in telling his stories to them. Carroll had a special gift for understanding children and cherished their curiosity and optimistic view of life. He also treasured their unprejudiced, innocent and carefree way of thinking.

He would take them out for trips on the river where the children loved the engaging, unusual stories that he made up as they went along, incorporating the children and the places they knew into the stories. One of the children, Alice Liddell, begged him to write down the story *Alice's Adventures in the Underground*. She was extremely persistent and kept on at him until he relented and in 1864 he presented her with a handwritten copy of the book as a Christmas gift. His peers quickly persuaded him to try and get it published and Macmillan instantly liked it. With the new title *Alice's Adventures in*

Wonderland, the book was published in 1865 and has been in print ever since.

The immediate success of the book was due to the fact that it contained some of the most imaginative things ever written, played with the limits of absurdity and was crammed with clever wordplay, logic puzzles and allegories. Carroll insisted his books were solely for entertainment purposes, but the underlying message was that you can indulge in fantasy if you want to and that you don't have to follow the rules if you don't want to. In other words, he was encouraging children to let their imagination run wild and suggesting that they could flourish by thinking differently; this was in direct contrast to the preaching, conforming and disciplined ideology typical of the authoritarian Victorian era.

Another reason *Alice's Adventures in Wonderland* was so popular, was that it was the first book to be written to appeal equally to adults and children. Hidden allegories, riddles and clever use of language were as entertaining to adults as the main story was fun and imaginative for children.

In a characteristic game of wordplay, the pen name he then adopted was conceived by translating his first two names, Charles Lutwidge, into latin, making *Carolus Ludovicus*, before reversing their order and retranslating them back into english to make Lewis Carroll.

Photography was another of his passions in an era when photography was just starting to establish itself as an art form. Being a lifelong gadget geek, he was fascinated by the technical demands of photography, as well as the precise, scientific aspects of the developing process. His pictures were very different to the traditional posed portraits that were typical of the time, as he was able to capture a more natural portrayal of his subjects. Exposure times could be as long as 45 seconds in the nineteenth century, so sitters had to remain perfectly still to avoid the picture being blurred.

This meant photographing children was particularly challenging, but Carroll kept them engaged by telling them stories. As a result, his photographs are considered to be some of the best examples of Victorian photography.

Throughout his life, he also had a profound interest in logic and wrote about it extensively, incorporating his unique flair to make it accessible to a wider audience. For example, take the classic case of symbolic logic where pairs of statements (premises) lead to a conclusion:

Premise A: Socrates is a man
Premise B: All men are mortal
Conclusion: Socrates is mortal

This was reworked by Carroll to be much more entertaining:

No bald creature needs a hairbrush
No lizards have hair
Conclusion: No lizard needs a hairbrush

In fact, he was working on symbolic logic just before his death and this manuscript wasn't found until the 1970s. It contained theories that were way ahead of their time and had it been published, he would probably have been regarded as one of the greatest British logicians of his era.

Autistic traits

Unconstrained by convention

Carroll's ability to delight children with his fantastical stories, puzzles, games and extraordinary poems portrays a man with a vivid and surreal imagination. His books for children were like nothing that had been written before. He not only captured the essence of a child's playful, make-believe world, but empowered Alice (the first female lead in children's literature) to challenge everything that she's expected to obey, encouraging his young readers to think for themselves rather than dutifully follow instructions. This was totally against the grain of how Victorian children were expected to behave and demonstrates Carroll's disdain for authority.

Unwilling to follow social rituals

In the *Alice* books Carroll repeatedly exposes what he sees as the absurdities of social convention, rules of etiquette and authority, which are all parodied. The banquet scene in *Through the Looking-Glass* is a great example of this; the Red Queen's obsession with etiquette and proper manners, to the point of depriving Alice of dinner, mocks the pretentious social rituals of Victorian society. This is typical of how autistic people view the illogical social world.

Novel thinker

As well as his extraordinary stories, Carroll was a keen inventor, always thinking up new ways of doing things. For example, his 'Memoria Technica' was a vastly improved way of remembering dates and formulae compared to the standard memory aids. He also invented the 'Nyctograph' – a novel stencil arrangement with a simplified alphabet for writing in the dark, so he could record thoughts that came to him when he woke up at night without the need to go through the lengthy process required to light a lamp.

Attention to detail and perfectionism

The original manuscript of *Alice's Adventures Underground* that Carroll presented to Alice as a gift was perfect in every respect. The completed handwritten book, with his precise and meticulous illustrations, contained no mistakes and was a superb example of his fastidious attention to detail.

John Tenniel, a professional illustrator and political cartoonist famous for his work in *Punch* magazine, produced the wonderful illustrations for the published book, however Carroll continually sent the pictures back requesting minor changes. He would not accept them until they were exactly as he wanted them to be.

Focus and persistence

He had relentless drive and determination, wrote mainly at a stand up desk and could do so by his own calculation for ten hours at a time. He was known to forget his meals and work into the night rather than have a break from what he was doing.

Special interests

From an early age, Carroll had a passion for word games and puzzles that he pursued his whole life and is one of the elements of the extraordinary appeal of the *Alice* books. He was always working on new ideas for games and actually invented an early form of the board game 'Scrabble' in 1880, writing in his diary "A game might be made of letters, to be moved about on a chess-board till they form words". [3] Photography, mathematics and logic were his other special interests and his exceptional expertise and innovation in these subjects is still acknowledged to this day.

Social difficulties

He struggled to make friends with adults, but felt at ease with children. It has been claimed that his life-long stammer was only evident when conversing with adults, yet he spoke fluently with children. Due to his stammer, he often pronounced his name "Do-do-do-dodgson" and so it's suspected that he named the Dodo character after himself. He certainly felt at his most comfortable with children, because they were honest and open and never judged him. Children say exactly what they think, whereas adults often don't say what they mean and can have a hidden agenda, which for someone with autistic tendencies can be confusing and illogical.

Caroll would openly speak his mind and as a result, many adults considered him to be rude and inflexible. His niece Violet Dodgson reported that "many found him difficult, exacting and uncompromising in business matters and in college life". [4]

Independent thought
It is clear that Carroll uses his own childhood propensity for independent thought and defiance of authority to define the character of Alice. Her concern with behaving correctly causes her distress, and she constantly struggles with rules, trying to follow the ones she finds acceptable and rejecting those she disagrees with.

Awkward appearance
He was a tall, rather gangly man with an ungainly gait and one shoulder higher than the other, giving him a decidedly awkward appearance. Being shy and retiring in the company of adults also tended to exaggerate this feature.

Literal interpretation
A popular anecdote about Carroll describes how Queen Victoria was apparently utterly charmed by *Alice's Adventures in Wonderland* and requested for "the next book Mr Carroll produces" to be sent to her.[5] His next book was *An Elementary Treatise on Determinants with their application to simultaneous linear equations and algebraical geometry* – she was not amused!

Logical

As well as his major contributions to logic in the field of mathematics, his logical way of thinking is strongly evident in the *Alice* books. Together with his skill in making up puzzles and riddles, he used these attributes to great effect in his writings. The appeal of nonsense literature is the *combination* of the sense with the non-sense, i.e. intertwining logic and the lack of logic by using wit and imagination. This is largely why his books appealed to both children and adults because the fun and fantasy captivated the younger readers, but the depth and intelligence of the writing was appreciated by adults.

Straightforward use of language

There are no long descriptive passages in Carroll's *Alice* books. He adopts a simplistic narrative style and sets out to tell a vivid story without the need for elaboration. An effective feature of his unique style is the frequent use of italics to *emphasise* a word. Most authors might use more descriptive words, but Carroll's simple use of italics makes sure the right words are emphasised to avoid confusion.

Strong sense of fairness

Carroll firmly believed in fairness for all and when Christ Church elected a governing body for the first time, he found himself voting on various issues. He developed an interest in the study of voting patterns, highlighted the failure of conventional voting methods and put forward some highly innovative proposals that were more just. His contribution to voting systems is still recognised and relevant today. For example, he proposed rules for fairer methods of eliminating players in lawn tennis tournaments years before the current seeding system was adopted.

Avid collector

He was fascinated by discoveries and inventions and amassed a large collection of gadgets, toys, games, puzzles and mechanical and technological inventions over his lifetime.

Meticulous record keeper

Throughout his adult life, Carroll kept a diary and although not every day is recorded, he wrote a detailed account of his activities. When in his late twenties, he began a register of all the letters he wrote and received, which totalled 98,721 in a 35 year period – more than seven per day. The letters ranged enormously in content from serious political and religious issues to light hearted nonsense. He also kept an accurate record of the 3,000 plus photographs that he took during his lifetime.

What has Lewis Carroll done for us?

Carroll revolutionised writing for children. Before his contributions, most children's books in the Victorian age were serious and used as a tool for teaching children about how to behave, with warnings of terrible things that might happen to them if they didn't follow instructions and obey the rules, e.g. *Grimms' Fairy Tales*. Instead, with his surreal imagination and wit, he made books fun and entertaining. This encouraged children to read and allowed them to let their own imaginations unfold.

The two *Alice* books also introduced the idea of making children's literature enjoyable for adults too – especially helpful as they were often the ones reading these stories to their children. He achieved this by including a wide variety of clever wordplay and riddles in his books, as well as providing stories that were open to interpretation, which I think captures the essence of all great art. For example, in the *Walrus and the Carpenter* poem, some people interpret the Walrus to be a caricature of the Buddha and the Carpenter to be a caricature of Jesus Christ, while others argue that the figures were political and that the Walrus and the Carpenter were an allegory for Britain and the United States.

Carroll was also a major inspiration for future fantasy authors – the seeds of his work can be seen blossoming into the likes of *The Wizard of Oz, The Hobbit, ET* and countless other creative works. Alice's adventures have spawned film, stage and music, with interpretations ranging from the fun and cheerful Walt Disney film, to the surreal Beatles Song *I am the Walrus*. Carroll's stories continue to resonate with and inspire all kinds of creative minds.

It's difficult to look back and comprehend just how groundbreaking and revolutionary his books were at the time. He developed a completely new approach to children's literature and, as a result, inspired future storytellers to open their minds to the wonderful world of imagination and fantasy, giving millions of children and adults alike endless hours of entertainment and pleasure.

Marie Curie (1867 - 1934)

Marie Curie's outstanding achievements all stem from her total absorption and obsessive interest in her work. She dedicated her whole life to science – her persistence was unswerving, particularly in an age when women were not even allowed to study at university in her home country. It was this ability to never give up, whatever the obstacles and personal sacrifices, that resulted in the hugely important discoveries she made in the fields of physics, chemistry and medicine.

Perseverance is a trait that many autistic people have, particularly when related to their special interests. I wouldn't begin to suggest that I'm in the same league as Marie Curie, but I did work hard at my piano skills, practicing every day without fail for over ten years before going to university. This has more than paid off, as I can now play at a professional level as well as with people who just play for fun. Having seen me perform, many people have relayed to me that they wish they "had stuck at piano lessons as a child" – demonstrating my persistence with the skill to be somewhat unique, or at least unusual. My propensity to 'stick at things' has put me in good stead with my judo too; I'm now a black belt and really enjoy being a member of a local club, as well as participating in competitions.

Why is she famous?

Marie Curie is famous for her pioneering work on radioactivity. She was the first woman to win a Nobel Prize and the only person ever to win Nobel Prizes in two different scientific fields, one in physics and the other in chemistry. Together with her husband, Pierre Curie, she discovered two new elements: polonium and radium. She then went on to develop the medical use of X-rays and worked on techniques in the use of radioactivity for the treatment of cancer. Her work launched a new era in medical research, diagnosis and treatment.

Childhood

Born Maria Sklodowska in Russian-occupied Poland, Marie was brought up by a family of intellects. Her mother was a gifted pianist and singer, and ran a prestigious Warsaw boarding school for girls, whilst her father was a physics and mathematics teacher – heavily influencing Marie's passions in life. From early on she displayed an obsessive curiosity and thirst for knowledge, so her father (keen to harness this) appointed himself as her mentor, positively encouraging her intellectual abilities.

Marie had a difficult childhood; when she was just eight years old her eldest sister tragically died of typhus and shortly after, her mother contracted tuberculosis. So afraid was her mother of passing the disease onto her children, that she refused to hug them and later died when Marie was only 10. This lack of physical touch no doubt influenced Marie's relationships with her own children.

Despite her tumultuous homelife, she was a keen student, avid reader and performed brilliantly at school. She also had an amazing memory and was often selected to recite poetry to visitors at her school, even though she was intensely shy and absolutely detested having to do this.

With her intense love for academia, university was the obvious next step after completing school, but the University of Warsaw's men only policy posed a stumbling block to her ambitions. The family wasn't well off enough to support her studying abroad, so she was forced to find an alternative way to follow her passion for the pursuit of science.

Adult Life

Living in an era when academic opportunities for women were few and far between, she continued her education at Warsaw's Uniwersytet Latający (floating university), an unofficial night school that ran informal classes. However, this simply wasn't sufficient to educate her to a high enough level, so to further her ambition to study at a top university, she and her sister Bronia formed a plan. Bronia would study medicine in Paris, where women were accepted, and Marie would work in private teaching to support her; Bronia would then return the favour once she had completed her studies. Marie thus spent the next five years working as a tutor, whilst continuing to study and learn at every opportunity.

Aged 24, she moved to France to join her sister where she could study physics and mathematics at the Sorbonne University of Paris. Marie (as she officially became known in France), rented a small attic to be close to the university, but had minimal resources. She kept herself warm in the cold winter months by wearing all the clothes she possessed, and at times survived solely on bread and butter with tea. Despite the hardships, this way of living meant she had total freedom to devote all her efforts to her studies and succeeded in gaining a physics degree in only two years, followed by a second degree in chemistry a remarkable one year later.

She may have had two degrees to her name, but Marie continued to study, taking on a research project in magnetism. Whilst looking for somewhere to conduct this research she met Pierre Curie, a physicist working in Paris who offered Marie space in his laboratory. They became friends through their common love of science, quickly got married and a year later their daughter Irene was born.

Still keen to continue her studies, Marie was looking for a topic for her PhD thesis. Wilhelm Röntgen had recently made the amazing discovery of a new type of ray that could pass through the human body and reveal the bones inside. He called them 'X' rays because nothing was known about them. The news of this remarkable discovery almost immediately caused a worldwide sensation.

A couple of months later, Henri Becquerel accidentally discovered another new ray that emitted from uranium salts – similar to Röntgen's X-rays, but much weaker. Although he presented his results to the scientific community there was little interest in his findings at the time because all their focus was on Röntgen's remarkable X-rays.

Marie decided that investigating these 'uranium rays' would be an excellent topic for her PhD. In order to do so, she needed to accurately measure the amount of radioactivity emitted by uranium. By amazing serendipity, Pierre had discovered the piezoelectric effect 16 years previously and now used it to invent a piezoelectric electrometer, which measured extremely low electrical currents and thereby enabled Marie to conduct her research.

Marie soon discovered that radiation was independent of molecular structure and therefore deduced that it must be linked to the interior of the atom itself. This was a radical new concept – the atom was then considered to be the most elementary particle (the word atom comes from the Greek word for indivisible) – and an absolutely revolutionary discovery.

Recognising how groundbreaking this discovery was, Pierre discontinued his own projects and proceeded to work with his wife. While studying the ore pitchblende, known for its uranium content, they discovered that it was far more radioactive than could be explained just by the uranium within it and concluded that another element must be present. This eventually led to their discovery of a new element: Polonium (named after her native country Poland). In 1898, only two years after she had commenced work on the project, it was added to the Periodic Table – a fabulous achievement for any scientist, let alone someone still in the middle of their PhD thesis. They also conceived the word 'radioactivity', inspired by the Latin 'radius', meaning ray.

However, Polonium still did not account for *all* of the additional radiation from pitchblende and further investigations led to the discovery of another radioactive element: Radium. The name reflects the fact that this new element was a million times more radioactive than uranium. They announced this discovery in a paper read to the French Academy of Sciences on 26 December 1898.

From 1898 to 1902, the Curies worked incredibly hard, putting superhuman effort into extracting tiny amounts of radium from literally tons of pitchblende for their experiments. Incredibly, during this period they also published a total of 32 scientific papers. Of note, one proposed that diseased, tumor-forming cells could be destroyed faster than healthy cells when exposed to radium which ultimately led to the development of new forms of cancer treatment.

In 1903 Marie submitted her doctorate thesis in physics entitled *Research on Radioactive Substances,* which became one of the most important scientific papers of the twentieth century. In what proved to be a splendid year, she and Pierre were awarded the Nobel Prize in Physics, together with Henri Becquerel, for the advances their studies of radiation made to the understanding of the structure of atoms.

The Curies' second daughter, Eve, was born in 1904. Devastatingly, just two years later, Pierre was killed in a street accident when he was knocked over by a horse and carriage. Shattered by his death, Marie further immersed herself in her work, as well as taking over Pierre's teaching position at the Sorbonne, becoming the university's first ever female professor.

Recognition of her work grew internationally and in 1910 she was awarded a second Nobel Prize – this time in chemistry, for the isolation of pure radium and the study of its nature and compounds. This enabled the prediction of about 30 new elements and showed that these elements undergo atomic transformations (what we now know as nuclear fission).

With the onset of the First World War, Marie put her research on hold and used her expertise in a practical capacity to help the war effort by designing small mobile X-ray units that could be used to diagnose injuries near the battlefront. Working with her 17 year old daughter Irene (who later went on to win a Nobel Prize too), they drove to the casualty clearing stations close to the front line to assist the surgeons by X-raying the wounded soldiers and locating the bullets, shrapnel and fractures. In addition to these mobile X-ray units, Marie also oversaw the construction of 200 radiological rooms at various fixed field hospitals behind the battle lines.

After the war, Marie focused her work on the medical uses of radiation, working and training students at the Radium Institute in Paris she had established just before the war. This was a major laboratory dedicated to the study of radiation and its uses. Her drive was always to promote science and education and she also founded the Warsaw Radium Institute where her sister Bronia became the Director. The 'Foundation Curie' was established in 1920 to fund the research and the first hospital opened in 1922, where innovative cancer treatments using radiation therapy were developed. These became a model for cancer centres around the world.

Marie died at the age of 66 of leukemia caused by her long-term exposure to radioactivity. All of her possessions, from research notes to cookbooks, are *still* radioactive and considered too dangerous to handle – they are kept in lead-lined boxes and anyone wishing to consult them must wear protective clothing. Her coffin too was lined with three layers of lead in order to contain the radiation.

In 1995, her remains (together with Pierre's) were re-interred in France's national mausoleum, the Pantheon, in Paris. Marie Curie thus became the first woman whose own accomplishments earned her the right to rest alongside France's most eminent people.

Autistic traits

Insatiable curiosity

Science was Marie's passion and her whole life was spent in pursuit of scientific knowledge. Her desire to understand aspects of the natural world through experimentation was driven by her intense curiosity and not necessarily by the need to solve a practical problem. As she said in a lecture she gave at Vassar College in 1921:

We must not forget that when radium was discovered no one knew that it would prove useful in hospitals. The work was one of pure science. And this is a proof that scientific work must not be considered from the point of view of the direct usefulness of it. It must be done for itself, for the beauty of science, and then there is always the chance that a scientific discovery may become like the radium, a benefit for humanity.[1]

Special Interest

Nothing could stand in her way when it came to pursuing her special interest in science. Marie had to tutor for five years before she could even attend university and continued to do so in the evenings when studying, all the while suffering a cold attic room and poor diet – the sacrifices being worth it in her eyes. Due to her total commitment and conviction, she succeeded in gaining her two science degrees in just three years. On occasion, she would be so focused that she would forget to eat.

She devoted her whole life to science with little regard for her health – clearly the Curies did not fully appreciate the danger of the radioactive materials they handled. Their working conditions were terrible. Health and safety today would never have allowed them to work as they did in a poorly ventilated building, which was little more than a shed, when processing tons of pitchblende to isolate the radium salts.

Dogged persistence

Marie simply never gave up, no matter how many obstacles were thrown at her. From having to battle at every opportunity to gain a scientific education, because she was female, to the difficulties she experienced gaining recognition in a male dominated profession, she persisted relentlessly.

Extracting the new element radium was a massive task requiring painstaking, laborious work. Tonnes of the uranium mineral pitchblende had to be processed to produce tiny amounts of radium (about 0.2g per tonne). Marie would handle 20kg batches of the mineral – grinding, dissolving, filtering, precipitating, collecting, redissolving, crystallising and recrystallising it to produce tiny quantities of the element. It was heavy and physically demanding work, which blackened and blistered her hands and made her feel ill (early signs of radiation sickness), but this did not deter her from her goal. She wrote "Sometimes I had to spend a whole day stirring a boiling mass with a heavy iron rod nearly as big as myself. I would be broken with fatigue at day's end".[2] In total, Marie and Pierre processed an immense sum of seven tonnes of pitchblende.

Intense focus
She had an innate power of concentration, so strong that no manner of distraction would cause her to redirect her attention – even the honour of receiving a Nobel Prize. Together with Pierre, they were awarded the Nobel Prize in Physics, but they declined to travel to Stockholm to accept the prize personally because it would interfere with their work.

Resolute determination
Marie requested funding from the French military in order to develop her mobile X-ray machines in WW1, but soon took the case in her own hands, frustrated by their slow response. She approached the Union of Women of France for money to produce the first mobile unit and then, using her scientific clout, asked wealthy Parisian women to donate vehicles. She soon had 20 vehicles, which she fitted out with the necessary X-ray equipment, trained 20 female volunteers and then set out to the frontline.

Strong sense of fairness
Marie had the opportunity to patent the technique for extracting radium from pitchblende and earn what could have been a considerable fortune, because radium therapy was becoming a recognised treatment for malignant tumours. However, Marie considered this to be "contrary to the scientific spirit" and did what she saw to be virtuous by releasing her findings with no economic gain.[3]

Dislike of social situations

She had no interest in socialising and was only ever truly happy when engrossed in her scientific pursuits. She met her husband through their scientific work and even when she was famous she disliked the attention it brought her, preferring to be immersed in her work. She considered science to be more interesting than people, saying "Be less curious about people and more curious about ideas".[4]

Emotionally detached

Marie was known to be so absorbed in her work that she had little capacity left for social niceties and hence came across as being cold and uncaring. Einstein said he had a deep friendship for her, but described her as "cold as a herring".[5]

This demeanor defined her in the family sphere too. Marie gave little of herself to her children – it was Pierre's father, a cheerful, playful man, who helped bring up the girls whilst their parents worked. She found it hard to express her affection for them, evidenced in Eve's biography of her mother, entitled *Madame Curie*. Eve claimed that to call her mother *Marie Curie* would have been too intimate, highlighting the distance between them both.

When Pierre died, Marie had no idea of her nine year old daughter Irene's despair, simply saying "she will soon forget completely".[6]

Although Marie didn't spend much time with her children, she made sure they got a good education and carefully monitored their development. She made detailed records of their growth, measuring the length of their arms, hands, head and legs rather like another scientific experiment.

Non-conformist

As an exclusively male profession, it was almost unheard of for a female to pursue a career in science in Marie's time, but Marie was not going to let social and cultural issues like this get in her way.

So much did science dictate her happiness that it even crept into romantic gestures. Pierre knew that the way to Marie's heart was through science (and not flowers), so gifted her an autographed copy of one of his physics papers to demonstrate his love for her. For their wedding, she opted to wear a dark blue suit purely so that she could wear it later in the lab.

What has Marie Curie done for us?

Marie Curie is an inspirational role model for females in science due to the enormous impact of her work on the world today. She pioneered the use of X- rays in medical diagnosis and during the war it is estimated that over a million soldiers were treated with her X-ray units. Her work led to the development of radiation therapy for the treatment of cancer and the Marie Curie charity in the UK is now a major organisation, which provides care and support to people with terminal illnesses, as well as their families.

Her list of achievements is hard to beat, but arguably her most profound breakthrough was her realisation that the atom was not the most elementary particle. This was a game-changing turning point in the development of our understanding of atomic physics and chemistry.

Sherlock Holmes

Although a fictional character, Sherlock Holmes is in fact based on a real person – as we shall see. Most importantly, he's an example of a character that most people are familiar with and who is admired *for* his autistic traits.

Holmes' predominant characteristic is his astonishing attention to detail; his ability to spot details that others miss. This is actually a very common autistic trait. For example, my parents got a new piano when I was about ten years old and upon first seeing it, I immediately said "there are three extra keys on the end" (the previous piano only had 85 keys). They were surprised that I'd noticed this, as it was 'just another piano' to them, but equally, I couldn't understand how they could possibly miss such an important detail.

People respect and admire Holmes due to his fine intellect and outstanding skills as a detective. Despite the fact that he comes across as rude and antisocial, any negative traits are tolerated and more than offset by his valuable contribution to society.

Why is he famous?
Sherlock Holmes is the world's most famous fictional consulting detective. He is known for his incredible powers of observation and

deduction, such that when the regular detectives in the police force were stumped by a case they called in Holmes, who used his extraordinary abilities to unravel the crime.

The first Sherlock Holmes stories were published in 1887 when London was being terrorised by the violent crimes of Jack the Ripper. Holmes became society's new hero due to his unique way of solving crimes and, with the advancements in printing and distribution at the time, his popularity quickly rose making him a household name.

In 2012, the character was awarded the world record for the most portrayed literary person in film and television. His popularity is due to his fascinating methods of solving the strangest and apparently inexplicable mysteries, which I put down to his autistic traits of logical thinking, immense attention to the tiniest detail, intense focus and dogged persistence.

How did he come about?
Sherlock Holmes was created by Sir Arthur Conan Doyle, who got the inspiration for Holmes' character in the form of his lecturer Dr. Joseph Bell, whilst studying medicine at Edinburgh University (1876-1881). Bell had extraordinary powers of deduction and taught his medical students the importance of close observation when making a diagnosis. He would study a patient's appearance in great detail and be able to accurately deduce factors such as their nationality, occupation and character and was usually able to describe their symptoms before the patient even had a chance to say a word. He would then make his diagnosis of the disease with incredible accuracy.

When Conan Doyle sent the first draft of his new detective story to Robert Louis Stevenson, author and fellow ex-student of Joseph Bell, he immediately wrote back saying "My compliments on your very ingenious and very interesting adventures of Sherlock Holmes. ... can this be my old friend Joe Bell?".[1]

Autistic traits

Phenomenal attention to detail

Holmes would spot things that had been totally overlooked by others. He doesn't just see things, he observes – pointing out that there is a big difference between the two. In fact, he says that he is able to see the "significance of trifles" and calls this his "method".[2]

In the television series featuring Benedict Cumberbatch, the cinematographers were able to employ special techniques, like extreme close ups (ECUs), to specifically demonstrate Holmes' focus on small details. For example, when Holmes is observing a male client, the frame zooms in on the top left hand side of the client's jacket and Holmes' deduction is 'unarmed', an ECU of his nail shows 'manicured', his thumb 'right handed', his shoe 'indoor worker', a hair on his trousers 'small dog', a different hair 'two small dogs'. They are all detailed observations that most people would simply not notice.

Extremely logical

One of his more memorable quotes was "Once you eliminate the impossible, whatever remains, no matter how improbable, must be the truth".[3] This is a perfect example of coming to a logical conclusion even though it may appear to be extremely unlikely.

Logic also dictated his views on marriage – he said that he would never marry as it would affect his work: "But love is an emotional thing, and whatever is emotional is opposed to that true cold reason which I place above all things. I should never marry myself, lest I bias my judgment". [4]

Intense focus and persistence

Sometimes he would not sleep for days when in the grips of a case and would often forget to eat. He describes a particularly difficult case as "a three pipe problem" – in other words, he knew it would take the time to smoke three whole meerschaum pipes worth of pure concentration to work on the solution. [5]

Special interests

Acquiring detailed knowledge about an obscure subject is a very typical autistic trait. Holmes has a deep knowledge of subjects such as criminology and chemistry, as well as some unusual topics like bees, ciphers, tattoos, lock picking, blood spatter analysis and tobacco ashes. In *The Sign of the Four*, Holmes says "I have been guilty of several monographs. They are all upon technical subjects. Here, for example, is one 'Upon the distinction between the Ashes of the Various Tobaccos'. In it I enumerate a hundred and forty forms of cigar, cigarette, and pipe tobacco, with coloured plates illustrating the difference in the ash". [6]

Prodigious memory for facts

Holmes has an exceptional memory which, together with his immense knowledge of the history of crime, means he can draw on a huge database of information to help him solve crimes. Dr. Watson notes that "he appears to know every detail of every horror perpetrated in the century". [7]

Unconstrained thinking

He has the ability to see a crime scene from multiple perspectives and refuses to be distracted by preconceived ideas, instead striving to look at problems from every possible angle. Conan Doyle's fictitious character succeeded in pioneering crime solving and forensic techniques that are common today, but were unheard of in the 1880s.

Tenacity

He would never give up and worked tirelessly until he had solved a crime. He also demonstrated this trait by becoming a skilled musician – he is an expert at playing the violin and says that music helps him think. For the same reason, he is also proficient in boxing and martial arts.

Direct manner

Holmes has a very direct manner – with no time for social niceties, or small talk – and is generally unconcerned about what people think about him. This means that he is perceived as being very blunt to the point of rudeness. However, it's clear that he's not intentionally trying to upset people, he simply wants to establish the facts and says exactly what he thinks.

In *The Hound of the Baskervilles*, for example, Mrs. Lyons seems quite shocked by the detective's manner, because "Holmes opened his interview with a frankness and directness which considerably amazed her".[8]

In *The Sign of Four*, Watson informs Holmes of his intention to marry and states that therefore this may be the last investigation in which they will work together. Holmes groans and says "I feared as much, I really cannot congratulate you".[9]

Socially insensitive

Holmes rarely follows social etiquette, tending to simply say what comes to his mind. For example, when Watson visits Holmes having not seen him for a while because he has recently married, Holmes doesn't greet him with a customary "Hello Watson, how is married life treating you?", but simply waves him to an armchair, throws across his case of cigars and says "Wedlock suits you, I think, Watson, that you have put on seven and a half pounds since I saw you".[10] As a result of his manner, which would appear to be unfriendly to anyone who did not understand him, Watson is his only friend.

Obsessive about his work

When Holmes solves the case of the Red-Headed League, he relates the quote "L'homme c'est rien – l'oeuvre c'est tout", translated "The man is nothing – the work is everything".[11] When working on a case, he was electric and totally engaged, but when at a loose end with no problems to solve, he was extremely melancholic to the point of being depressed. In *The Red-Headed League* he says "My life is spent in one long effort to escape from the commonplaces of existence. These little problems help me to do so".[12]

Sensory issues

Holmes has a heightened awareness of certain smells, tastes and textures, which at times, provides him with extra insight and clues at a crime scene. However, some loud noises cause him actual pain, highlighting an extreme sensory sensitivity.

Self stimulating (stimming) behaviour

Holmes has a habit of pacing up and down his room when he is thinking. Both Dr. Watson and his landlady, Mrs. Hudson, comment on his continual pacing, sometimes right through the night. He also had a habit of "wriggling in his chair" when he was excited about a case.[13]

What has Sherlock Holmes done for us?

The Sherlock Holmes stories have sold more than 60 million copies, been translated into over 100 languages and made into over 50 movies and TV programmes. Anyone who wants to learn about autism could start by reading some of the stories as he certainly had a lot of autistic traits.

Holmes would have been perceived very differently if he was portrayed as autistic first, rather than detective first. Autistic people are often stigmatised in a world dominated by social skills, but put us in a situation where social skills aren't of prime importance and you could see us in a completely different light – judged by how good we are at what we *can* do instead. Holmes is a perfect example, a role model even, of why employers should take on autistic people. Despite having to make allowances for our atypical behaviour, the benefits can hugely outweigh any disadvantages.

So, what has Sherlock Holmes done for us? Looking at him through my autistic lens, he showcases a most important message: the fact that autistic people can be entertaining, interesting and valuable members of society.

Albert Einstein (1879 – 1955)

There is no doubt that Einstein had a unique way of thinking. He is the ultimate example of how a different way of thinking can lead to entirely new ideas. His individual approach challenged the accepted laws of physics, which had been the standard for the previous few hundred years. He is known for his famous 'thought experiments', where he could take a complex physics problem and boil it down to a simple visual image. It was this phenomenal visual thinking ability that was directly responsible for his groundbreaking discoveries.

Although known for being a world famous physicist, he once said that if he hadn't been a scientist, he would have pursued a career as a musician. Einstein was taught to play the piano and violin when he was very young by his mother, who was an accomplished pianist in her own right, and music played an important part throughout his life. "Music helps him when he is thinking about his theories", said his wife Elsa, "He goes to his study, comes back, strikes a few chords on the piano, jots something down, returns to his study".[1]

Music can be attractive to autistic people, because it's logical and rule bound. I too studied physics and am a musician, so I fully understand the relationship. In my case it also helps to overcome social deficiencies. People regularly come up to me after a performance to discuss music, which is great for me because we're engaging about a specific interest of mine (which I'm good at), rather than just small talk (which I'm hopeless at).

Why is he famous?

Einstein has to be the most famous scientist ever, primarily because of his mind-blowing theory of relativity, which linked space, time and gravity. Working entirely alone and using only pencil, paper and the sheer power of his mind, he devised a theory which revolutionised our understanding of how the universe works and changed everything that physicists thought they knew about the universe at the time. It is without doubt the single greatest scientific idea ever conceived.

Childhood

German born Albert Einstein was, as one would imagine, an intensely curious child. The world is a fascinating place for most, but even its everyday intricacies enthralled young Einstein. Yet interestingly, despite his obvious intelligence, he was notably late learning to speak; so much so that his parents consulted a doctor. This turned out to be a conscious decision made by young Einstein, who preferred to soak up his surroundings rather than comment on them.

Not understanding his idiosyncrasies, other children just perceived him as 'different' and would make fun of him; this exacerbated Einstein's tendency to entertain himself rather than try and socialise, so he spent much of his childhood alone. He didn't need to communicate with books and took great solace in the knowledge that they would impart, choosing to spend the majority of his time reading and particularly enjoying anything about the natural world. When not reading, he would get stuck into a puzzle and loved any kind of trick, or game. Aged nine, he spent hours painstakingly building a tower of cards a phenomenal 14 stories high, showcasing his unshakable focus even as a young child.

His father, who manufactured electrical equipment for a living, enthusiastically encouraged Einstein's interest in science. On one occasion, he gave him a compass, which totally fascinated Einstein and led to his lifelong passion of wanting to understand how things can be forced to move even though nothing is touching them. He became gripped by a desire to understand the underlying laws of nature and was further inspired by a series of science books by Aaron Bernstein. These books contained vivid pictures and diagrams to help understand physics and asked questions such as 'What would a trip through space be like?' and 'What would it be like to travel through an electrical wire?'. It even mentioned the constant speed of light, a subject which became a central topic of Einstein's theory of relativity. As a young child, with a thirst for knowledge and an open mind, this method of thinking visually and imagining situations appealed immensely and ultimately became a defining feature of Einstein's thought processes for the rest of his life.

Even as a child, he took nothing for granted, questioned everything and never blindly accepted the prevailing or traditional explanation for things. He was keen to understand not just why things happen, but would also ask the question 'How do we know what we know?'. Thus he developed an interest in philosophy and as a teenager, he read all three of Immanuel Kant's major works.

Aged only 16, one of the critical thought experiments he began to play with was trying to imagine what would happen if you could catch up with a light wave – what would you see? He would pace up and down and it would actually cause him so much anxiety that his palms would sweat. This wasn't an ordinary curiosity, this was an overwhelming and passionate desire to not only understand, but get to the bottom of the question.

A propensity for excellence at maths and science at school was equally offset by being very poor at other subjects, simply because they just didn't interest him. School was boring, he disliked the method of teaching and rebelled against the authoritarian attitude of some of his teachers. He preferred to work things out for himself and play with ideas and equations on his own rather than learn things by memory in a school classroom. His teachers were unimpressed by this individuality and thought he was lazy – his school master even said he thought he would never amount to anything (how ironic!). However, when something sparked his interest, he would display immense powers of concentration and focus; autistic traits which would ultimately lead to his revolutionary discoveries.

After school he enrolled on a four-year teaching diploma, specialising in maths and physics, but, as usual, missed most of his classes because he didn't like the style of teaching. Instead, he spent much of his time sitting in the Cafe Metropole in Zurich reading the works of the great philosophers. If not for his friends' class notes, he might never have graduated. His professors found him a bit too full of himself and responded by giving him negative job references. Laboratory directors across Europe would later have to live down the fact that they had rejected job applications from *the* Albert Einstein.

Adult Life

Aged 23, he started work at the patent office in Bern, Switzerland, where his job was to assess the originality of new inventions. This was the era of electrification, so lots of completely new ideas were passing through his office. Time zones had recently been introduced in central Europe and accurately synchronising clocks was a major challenge of the day. Switzerland was a world leader in time technology and many patents to link clocks were brought to Einstein's attention. Because of his intense focus, he would complete a normal day's work processing patent applications in just two or three hours and would then set to work on his physics theories. Fortunately, owing to the quality and accuracy of his work, his boss was very indulgent and turned a blind eye to this.

In 1905, aged just 26, he published not just one but four of the most visionary scientific papers ever written; a remarkable feat given that he came up with them purely by sitting and thinking them through by himself. The first of these four papers won Einstein his Nobel Prize. It explained the causes of the photoelectric effect and proposed the most original scientific idea of the twentieth century: quantum theory. The concept that light must not only travel in waves (energy), but also exist as particles (matter) would be the seed of one of the main pillars of modern physics: quantum mechanics.

The second paper mathematically proved the existence of atoms and molecules. His use of statistical fluctuations and probability theory in that paper eventually revolutionised the study of all complex systems – weather, climate, stock markets, and evolution, to name a few – and forever improved our understanding of how the world works. The findings were revolutionary and if he had only published this single paper, he would have gone down in history. Einstein's calculations were later fully confirmed by Jean Perrin who, in 1926, won a Nobel Prize *just* for proving that Einstein's 1905 paper was correct.

The third was his theory of special relativity which unified space and time into a single concept: spacetime. One consequence of this is that time slows the faster we move – hence astronaut Scott Kelly, who spent six months on the International Space Station travelling at 17,000 miles per hour, returned to earth 13 milliseconds younger than his twin brother.

The fourth paper was, in effect, an epilogue of all the other papers. It provided mathematical proof of special relativity and, therefore, the confirmation that mass and energy are interchangeable, which condenses into the most famous equation in history: $E = mc^2$.

Despite these amazing achievements, it took time for the scientific community to recognise the significance of his work and so it wasn't until 1909 that he was finally able to secure an academic post as a professor at Zurich University. He was now able to work on modifying his special theory of relativity to include acceleration and gravity. He worked almost non-stop for the next six years with little regard for sleep, time off at the weekend, or holidays. But this wasn't work as far as Einstein was concerned, it was pure passion – reminding me of the saying 'find a job you enjoy and you'll never have to do a day's work in your life'.

He finally made his breakthrough in his general theory of relativity in 1915. It totally changed physicists' views of gravity and is considered by many to be one of *the* great moments in the history of science. However, when Einstein presented his great theory, few people understood it, or even believed it. He needed astronomers to conduct a practical test in order to prove to the world that the counterintuitive features of his theory were real.

In 1919, an English astronomer, Arthur Eddington, led an expedition to the African island of Principe to measure how much a star's light would bend around the massive body of the sun during a total eclipse. This happened exactly as predicted and proved that Einstein's theory was correct. Only then did Einstein become a worldwide celebrity.

By 1920, the two most famous people in the western world were Charlie Chaplin and Albert Einstein, who went on to become great friends. Chaplin reportedly said to Einstein "The only reason they all love me is because they understand everything I do, and the reason they all love you is they don't understand anything you do".[2]

Autistic traits

Curiosity

Einstein once said "I have no special talent. I am only passionately curious".[3] Curiosity was without doubt his motivation for pursuing physics. He summed this up neatly when he said "One cannot help but be in awe when one contemplates the mysteries of eternity, of life, of the marvellous structure of reality".[4]

On the other hand, he could be lazy and obstinate when a matter didn't interest him. Nonetheless he had an intense passion for understanding the things "the ordinary adult never bothers his head about".[5] Curiosity was, in his opinion, the greatest reason for his accomplishments – he recognised that "love is a better teacher than a sense of duty".[6]

Visual thinker

Einstein's thought experiments were the key to his success. He would stare out of the window while working at the patent office thinking about how things move in space and time. For example, he imagined being on a train travelling at the speed of light and looking back at the apparently stationary hands of a clock as the train travelled away from it. This led him to realise that time changes according to the speed of the observer and was the spark of inspiration for his theory of special relativity.

Logical thinking

Whilst essential for his maths and physics work, his logical way of thinking also meant that he was perceived to be eccentric in everyday life. For example, he often would not wear any socks, even to formal occasions. Logic dictated that if the big toe caused a hole to appear in your socks, then why wear socks at all? The logic of not wearing socks superseded, for him, the logic of conforming to social etiquette.

He also did not like to waste any time or mental energy on unimportant matters and hence had a remarkably messy room and equally messy desk. When asked about this, he said "If a cluttered desk is a sign of a cluttered mind, of what, then, is an empty desk a sign?"[7] Einstein wanted to conserve all of his brain power for creative tasks so, for example, he had multiple sets of identical clothes which meant that he didn't need to expend any thought whatsoever on deciding what to wear each day.

Out of the box thinking

Einstein is a classic case of having the ability to think outside the box and not to be constrained by how others think. Most people considered the laws of physics, going back to Isaac Newton in the 1600s, to be set in stone and that future progress in physics would need to build on these solid foundations. It was in Einstein's nature however, to question absolutely everything and take nothing for granted. He was a completely independent thinker with no preconceptions, or regard for conventional methods.

It was this way of thinking that enabled him to come up with the idea that time itself might not be fixed, something that everyone else took for granted. If that's not out of the box thinking, I don't know what is. As Einstein himself said "Logic will get you from A to B. Imagination will take you everywhere".[8]

Focus

Einstein's lifelong interest in understanding the universe led to him at times working like a man obsessed – his focus was so intense that he would often forget to eat, or sleep. This was his passion, so it wasn't 'work'. He was at his happiest when he was devoting time to complex problems, trying to make sense of the world.

He also had an incredible ability to remain focused on the task in hand despite being distracted by his surroundings. His son reported: "Even the loudest baby-crying didn't seem to disturb Father," adding, "He could go on with his work completely impervious to noise".[9] His first PhD pupil, Hans Tanner, gave a graphic picture of his supervisor's ability to focus:

> He was in his study in front of a heap of papers covered with mathematical formulae. Writing with his right hand and holding his younger son in his left, he kept replying to questions from his elder son Hans Albert who was playing with his bricks. With the words "Wait a minute, I've nearly finished," he gave me the children to look after for a few moments and went on working. It gave me a glimpse into his immense powers of concentration.[10]

Persistence

A defining quality of Einstein was his persistence. Many considered him to be a genius, however he did not think so and once said "It's not that I'm so smart, it's just that I stick with problems longer".[11] General relativity didn't come in one 'eureka' moment but in a long, sustained effort over many years. Right up to the end of his life he was continually writing out equations, trying to come up with answers and simply never giving up.

Social difficulties

Einstein had little interest in the social world, partly because he was happy spending most of his time working on his theories and partly because he didn't feel the need to socialise. "Although I am a typical loner in daily life, my consciousness of belonging to the invisible community of those who strive for truth, beauty, and justice has preserved me from feeling isolated".[12]

Despite this, he did marry and his wife Elsa was initially attracted to him by his music playing skills, saying "I fell in love with Albert because he played Mozart so beautifully on the violin. I was so entranced by the beautiful melodies that I could hardly keep my eyes off of him".[13]

Late talker

Albert Einstein was a very late talker. At the dinner table one evening, he finally broke his long silence. "The soup is too hot," he complained. His parents, greatly relieved, asked him why he had never spoken before. "Because" he replied, "up to now everything has been okay". [14]

Language delay is often the first sign of autism. I too didn't start talking until I was three, which was why I was then sent for assessment. Einstein's parents were similarly concerned about his development – if only they knew what was in store for him!

Irreverence

The well known picture of Einstein sticking his tongue out at the camera is a good example of his irreverence – not the sort of behaviour one would normally expect from such a respected academic.

People's status did not concern Einstein in the slightest. "I speak to everyone in the same way, whether he is the garbage man or the president of the university". [15]

From an early age he was a rebel, a loner and always wanted to learn in his own way. He disliked the traditional methods of schooling that required memorising reams of boring facts and hated the authoritarian attitude of some of his teachers. He often missed classes altogether and would instead study theoretical physics at home. By the age of 12, encouraged by his parents who had bought him an advanced mathematical textbook to study during the summer holidays, he was already solving complicated maths problems. Einstein thus learned his physics not at school, but by obsessively puzzling over ideas and equations by himself.

Later in life, Einstein acknowledged his irreverence and said: "To punish me for my contempt for authority, fate made me an authority myself". [16]

What has Albert Einstein done for us?

Einstein's theories revolutionised our understanding of the world around us – from the smallest of things (proving that atoms and molecules exist), through to explaining the biggest (gravity, space, time and the universe).

His work contributed to many technologies that play a big part in our day-to-day lives. Quantum mechanics led to the development of the semiconductor and thus the transistor, which in turn became the microprocessor that lies at the heart of our computer-based society.

General relativity, which tells us that time is not fixed, has enabled us to build satellite navigation technology that provides the positioning data for the navigation of cars, ships and planes on a global basis. GPS simply wouldn't work if we failed to make adjustments for the time difference between the clocks on satellites and receivers on the ground.

His Nobel Prize winning paper about the photoelectric effect has contributed to the technologies responsible for lasers and photoelectric cells. The applications of these are too numerous to mention, but include, for example, fibre optics, solar panels, scanners, DVDs, automatic doors and digital cameras.

But, the really big thing has to be $E = mc^2$. This led directly to nuclear fission, the physics behind the atomic bomb and nuclear power. Also, until Einstein deduced $E = mc^2$ it was a complete mystery as to what the fuel source of the Sun was (nuclear fusion). A measure of how important this could be for the future of mankind is reflected in how much governments are now spending on nuclear fusion research. The International Thermonuclear Experimental Reactor (ITER), based in France, is the world's largest fusion experiment. Started in 2013, it is the most expensive science experiment in history with a projected cost of $65 billion and counting.

If it works, and I'm optimistic that it will, nuclear fusion will become the predominant clean energy source for mankind, end our reliance on fossil fuels and save us from the looming disaster of climate change. This will all be as a direct result of Einstein.

Ludwig Wittgenstein (1889 – 1951)

Communication is probably the key issue that autistic people have to deal with when talking with neurotypicals (and vice-versa). In my first book, *It's Raining Cats and Dogs*, I outlined why autistic people have difficulties with common phrases, idioms and metaphors – the whole issue of the complexities of our bizarre language is further explored in my second book, *A Different Kettle of Fish*.

Ludwig Wittgenstein was one of the most famous philosophers of the last century and his work was largely about the difficulties of language as a means of communication. His work is extraordinarily hard for anyone to understand and to this day philosophers, among others, still argue about what he actually meant. Even though most of his work goes way over my head, some of it is accessible to me, because I can see many examples of 'autistic thinking' when reading about his life and ideas. I found that I kept saying to myself "oh yes, I do that", or "that's exactly how I think". Clearly, we have a few things in common.

Wittgenstein pointed out that words have different meanings according to the context in which they are used. I often hear words that seem completely illogical to me, and therefore simply 'don't compute' in my mind, yet seem perfectly understandable to neurotypicals. On a daily basis I hear totally inappropriate use of words, for example the instruction: "go through the door and it's on the right". I'd be interested to know how you actually *go through* a solid door without causing a lot of damage!

He also proposed that language is a game at which some players are more skilled than others. This is where autistic people can struggle. Neurotypical people understand the rules of language and social interaction, whereas for us they are not built in – we don't instinctively know the rules and hence we are perceived as outsiders, oddballs, or non-participants. This is one of the main problems facing autistic people in the neurotypical world.

I have found that engaging in group activities helps me to overcome these social challenges, which are often caused by language issues. From playing music in a band to joining clubs (judo, rock climbing etc.), being part of a 'tribe' makes communication far more accessible to me, as we are all speaking the same language about the common ground that we share. I can also discuss data analysis with my other team members at work all day long without any problems at all.

What's so fascinating about Wittgenstein, from my point of view, is that it seems to me that he was trying to get to the bottom of why it was so difficult for him, a highly intelligent individual, to communicate and socialise with ordinary people; his articulation of the problems of communication he himself experienced give us a glimpse into the workings of the autistic brain. In other words, he's telling us about his own autistic way of thinking.

Why is he famous?
Wittgenstein was an Austrian philosopher who is acknowledged to be one of the most original and influential philosophers of the twentieth century. He is revered as one of the intellectual giants of the time – in the same league as people such as Albert Einstein,

Sigmund Freud and Alan Turing. His books *Tractatus* and *Philosophical Investigations* were ground-breaking and laid many of the foundations of how logic and philosophy are understood today.

Wittgenstein felt he could revolutionise the notoriously complicated and ambiguous world of philosophy by making it logic based. Whether he succeeded or not is still a matter of opinion.

Childhood

Wittgenstein was born in 1889 into one of the wealthiest families in Austria – his father being a major figure in the iron and steel industry. He was the youngest of nine children and the family was at the centre of Viennese artistic and cultural life.

All of the children were musical. Brahms (the German, Romantic era composer and pianist) was a family friend and the home had a total of seven grand pianos. All of his siblings pursued music with obsessive enthusiasm and young Ludwig himself had perfect pitch; apparently he could whistle long pieces of music with great accuracy and expression. He said that music was so essential to him that he could hardly put into words its enormous importance. [1]

During his formative years, Wittgenstein was privately educated at home and demonstrated practical skills from an early age – when he was just 10, he constructed a working model of a sewing machine made out of bits of wood and wire. All of his siblings went on to grammar school, but aged 14, Wittgenstein was sent to a technical school in Vienna because he appeared to be more technically minded rather than academic and it was feared that he would not pass the rigorous entrance exams set by the grammar school.

Due to his lack of social skills and privileged background, Wittgenstein didn't fit in at the school and was immediately unpopular – he dressed elegantly and spoke to his peers using the very formal Hochdeutsch language (literally meaning 'high German', a loose equivalent of the Queen's English). This inevitably led to ridicule and bullying, and his peers would tease him incessantly by chanting a little rhyme they had made up about how different, and how unhappy he was: "Wittgenstein wandelt wehmütig widriger Winde wegen Wienwarts", translating to "Wittgenstein wends his woeful windy way towards Vienna". [2]

His school reports survive and show that on the whole he was a fairly poor student gaining grades equivalent to a C or D in most subjects.

Adult Life

In 1906, Wittgenstein was sent to a technical college in Berlin and developed an interest in the then very young science of aeronautics. But, despite his scientific interests, he would spend a lot of his spare time contemplating philosophical questions. Two years later, he went on to study aeronautical engineering in England at Manchester University and it was here that the seeds of his interest in philosophy began to grow. This was a pivotal point in his life, which marked the beginning of the transformation from being a mediocre student (at best) to one at the very top of his field.

He found himself questioning the very concepts of the maths he was being taught and, delving into this further, he came across Bertrand Russell's 1903 book *The Principles of Mathematics*. He became so obsessed with the questions of mathematical logic that he dropped his studies in aeronautics and in 1911, went to Cambridge to study the philosophy of mathematics and logic with Bertrand Russell himself. Russell was deeply impressed by Wittgenstein's advanced thought, describing him as "perhaps the most perfect example I have ever known of genius as traditionally conceived, passionate, profound, intense and dominating". [3]

He worked so intensely and with such focused preoccupation that only a year later, the 23 year old knew so much logic that Russell believed he had nothing left to teach him. Wittgenstein, on the other hand, believed he still had a way to go – he struggled with the fact that he couldn't get right into the heart of his most fundamental questions about logic.

The environment at Cambridge was too socially intense and disturbing for him and therefore, in 1913, he moved to Norway to work alone in remote isolation in a hut he had built by the side of a fjord. This enabled him to pursue his passion in logic with minimal distractions and in complete seclusion. His mountain cabin, set in picturesque Skjolden, has since been rebuilt and is now open to visitors.

In the summer of 1914 Wittgenstein returned to visit his family in Vienna. During this visit Austria declared war on Serbia and, despite not being liable for military service due to health issues, he volunteered and was assigned to an artillery regiment in Krakow. He actively participated in the Galician campaign in 1914 and was then called to the Russian front in 1916. Wittgenstein seemed to approach World War One as a personal test, being of the belief that he would only discover his full worth by facing death. During the war, he endeavoured to reach the front line in pursuit of maximum danger and would volunteer for service at the artillery observation post at night so as to expose himself to the greatest risk possible.

Throughout the war, Wittgenstein continued his philosophical thinking and, perhaps not surprisingly, his focus progressed from logic to reflections on ethics, death and the meaning of life. During a period of leave in the summer of 1918 he completed the manuscript of his first book *Tractatus Logico-philosophicus*. After the war ended, *Tractatus* was published and well received as a major step forward from previous philosophical work on the nature of logic.

Tractatus explored the inadequacy of language as a means of communication and proposed that there is a difference between reality and the spoken word trying to describe it – a difference that partly stems from our different experiences, which causes us to each build our own 'dictionaries'. For example 'heavy' snowfall to someone in London might mean six inches of snow, whereas to someone in Alaska it might mean six feet. If language was perfect, i.e. if it was purely logical, then everything said would be clearly either true or false. In other words language is extremely sloppy, to the point that different words mean different things to different people. Words also have different functions dependent on the context in which they're used, meaning we don't just use words to make statements of fact. "In most cases, the meaning of a word is its use", he claimed. [4]

As far as he was concerned, *Tractatus* had solved all philosophical problems. So, in 1920 he gave up philosophy, gave away his part of the family fortune to his siblings and took on various different jobs in and around Vienna, including gardening, teaching and architecture. During this time, he continued discussing the philosophy of mathematics and science with various intellectual friends in Vienna. These discussions eventually rekindled his passion in philosophy, such that he decided to return to Cambridge in 1929 to resume his philosophical vocation.

Over the next few years his conception of the problems of philosophy underwent dramatic changes, so much so that he rejected his own previous work in *Tractatus*. During the 1930s, Wittgenstein conducted seminars at Cambridge and worked on developing the new ideas that he intended to publish in his second book, *Philosophical Investigations*. In 1939 he was elected Professor of Philosophy at Cambridge and Fellow of Trinity College, but although most of his colleagues respected his genius and tolerated his eccentricity, they regarded him as withdrawn, mysterious, inaccessible – somewhat mad even.

In 1945 he prepared the final manuscript of *Philosophical Investigations*, but curiously only authorised its posthumous publication. In it, Wittgenstein rejects his own earlier theory of language, as outlined in *Tractatus*, and forms an entirely new one. As he said "Philosophy is not a theory but an activity". [5] This new approach to language was eventually called ordinary language philosophy, and looked at language as a kind of social game. This shifted the emphasis from a theoretical formal language to everyday language and its actual use.

For a few more years, he continued his philosophical work and travelled during this period to the United States and Ireland. Legend has it that on his deathbed, which was as a result of cancer in 1951, his last words were "Tell them I've had a wonderful life". [6]

Autistic traits

Independent thinker
Wittgenstein was not prepared to blindly accept what he was taught, but always questioned everything and wanted to work things out for himself from first principles. When studying aeronautical engineering at Manchester, he soon found himself questioning the underlying concepts of the maths he was being taught. Most people accept mathematical formulae as working tools that everyone uses, so what's the point in questioning them, but autistic people don't 'follow the crowd', they think for themselves.

Logical thinker
Bertrand Russell, widely considered to be one of the twentieth century's premier logicians, said that Ludwig Wittgenstein knew so much logic that he had nothing left to teach him after just one year.

Trying to apply logic to the complex field of philosophy, which is extremely open to different interpretations and not at all clear cut, was a phenomenal task to undertake. However, Wittgenstein was such an obstinately logical thinker that he attempted this task in *Tractatus*.

The book is about understanding the logic of language. He is trying to show that the way that philosophers formulate traditional philosophical problems is confused, because they misunderstand the logic of language. He wanted the book to help philosophers come to an understanding of the logic of language, and he believed that this would result in all of the major problems of philosophy being solved.

It was his autistic way of thinking that meant he was ideally placed to investigate this, because he *thought* logically, but was forced to *use* illogical language.

Intense passion

According to Bertrand Russell, Wittgenstein was "full of boiling passion which may drive him anywhere". [7] Russell came increasingly to identify with Wittgenstein as a fellow thinker, who brought all his force and passion to bear on theoretical questions: "He has more passion about philosophy than I have; his avalanches make mine seem mere snowballs. He is addicted to passionately intense thinking". [8]

Stating the obvious

Some autistic people can be very good at pointing out what is obvious in complex situations and it seems to me that Wittgenstein had this ability. He used it to point out that one of the fundamental problems of philosophy is that language use is not logical. As language is the tool used to discuss philosophy, we need to work out a logical basis for language before we can then move on to address philosophy.

Repetitive behaviours/Liked sameness

Wittgenstein would spend a great deal of time arranging and rearranging his philosophical works and transferring them from one copy book to another. He liked to listen to the same piece of music over and over again, and he always dressed in the same way. On visiting Norman Malcolm, a former student, he enjoyed the rye bread and cheese he had for his first lunch so much that he would eat nothing else during his stay. He declared that it did not matter to him what he ate so long as it was always the same. [9]

Social difficulties

He was feared in Cambridge because of his shocking frankness and lack of any social graces, and he had great difficulty in managing social relationships, explaining that human relations were like Chinese to him.[10]

He hated small talk. He had a horror of certain kinds of language, in particular "idle talk and unintelligibility"; in other words, talk that lacked substance, or failed to produce meaning. [11] Of course, if you're neurotypical, small talk has value. It enables each party to judge the other's mood and willingness to continue social interaction. It has been suggested that about 70% of communication is non-verbal – body language, tone of voice, etc. – therefore small talk is the perfect opportunity to focus on these other aspects of communication. In other words, the actual language used is just a filler dedicated to understanding the other person's non-verbal cues. Most autistic people can't see the point of meaningless small talk – to us it's like verbal diarrhoea – and Wittgenstein was clearly no exception.

His social difficulties were further compounded by his somewhat strange appearance. He had "extremely penetrating eyes", and there was "something peculiar about his gait". [12]

Communication difficulties

He experienced great difficulty in communicating with people, saying he never felt he was understood even by those who professed to be his disciples. He doubted he would be better understood in the future and once said he felt as though he was writing for "people who would think in a different way, breathe a different air of life, from that of present-day men". [13]

Extremely blunt

Wittgenstein could whistle whole movements of symphonies with great accuracy, but when other people whistled something wrong he would stop them and firmly tell them how it should go.

For his PhD thesis, he submitted *Tractatus* to his examiners Professor Bertrand Russell and Professor G E Moore, two of the most brilliant minds of the time. He spent a few minutes trying, but failing, to explain *Tractatus* to them, then stood up, patted them both on the back and said "Don't worry, you'll never understand it". [14]

Liked solitude

His motivation for moving to Skjolden in 1913, the remote village in Norway, was to allow him to concentrate on his work. Here, he was away from society and free from the kind of obligations and expectations that were part and parcel of the bourgeois life that he felt was imposed upon him in both Cambridge and Vienna (e.g. what he saw as frivolous concerns about wealth and respectability, which he considered banal and trivial). His intense dislike of these mindsets was based in part on the superficial nature of the relationships it created. In Skjolden, he could be free from such conflicts; isolation allowed him to be himself without the strain of upsetting or offending people. It was a tremendous liberation. He could devote himself entirely to himself – or rather, what he felt to be practically the same thing, to his logic.

Speech problems

Wittgenstein was a late talker, not speaking until he was four years old, and issues with speech continued into his adult years.

Sometimes his brain would work so fast that he couldn't get the words out – he would often begin to stammer while attempting to address a group of colleagues, for example. Eventually, his stuttering would give way to a tense silence, during which he would struggle mutely with his thoughts, gesticulating all the while with his hands, as if he was still speaking audibly. "He keeps interrupting himself. Arguing with himself. You're hearing one of the most amazing dialogues for one that you could ever imagine", a colleague recalled.[15]

Obsession with detail
When he published *Tractatus*, Wittgenstein thought that it was the last work of Philosophy that would ever need to be written, so he looked around for how to fill the rest of his life. He turned to architecture and spent a couple of years designing a house for his sister in Vienna. During the project, he became consumed by the smallest of details, like getting the door handles and the radiators right. Very late on in the process, he got increasingly bothered about the ceiling in one of the rooms and came to the conclusion that it was too low. At immense inconvenience to everyone he insisted on having it raised by 3cm. It made all the difference, he thought.

What has Ludwig Wittgenstein done for us?
It's not often that most of us think about philosophy, or why it might be important to us. Yet ultimately, philosophers encourage us to think critically about the world and are the foundation of all knowledge.

Aristotle (350 BC) wrote the earliest Western textbooks on a wide variety of topics including physics, biology, ethics, rhetoric and art – all based on his theory of Philosophical Logic. Over the next 2,000 years philosophy blossomed until, it seems to me, Wittgenstein came along and basically said that it's all very well discussing these things, but the same words have different meanings to different people. So, unless we sort out this problem first then any other attempts at philosophy are futile. He proposed that the way previous philosophers had addressed philosophical questions were not representative of true life because they thought philosophical problems were to do with understanding the nature of the world, whereas Wittgenstein thought they were to do with language – the means people use to convey the problems.

His different way of thinking approached philosophy from an entirely new angle and provided a solid foundation for the future development of philosophy, and thus human intellect itself.

What has Wittgenstein done for our understanding of autism?

As described above, Wittgenstein helped the development of philosophy by pointing out that we have to be very careful about the language we use to discuss philosophical concepts.

I believe he has also achieved another important thing: due to his autistic way of thinking, he has explained (to me at least) why autistic people struggle with social communication.

In a nutshell, the two big problems are:

1. "The meaning of a word is its use"[4] - i.e. the same word can have multiple meanings depending on the context it is used in. This explains why idioms and metaphors are so difficult for autistic people; we think logically and try to work out the meaning of the idiom by looking at the meaning of the words used.

2. For autistic people, language is a tool to convey information, however for neurotypicals, language is often used for social game playing. This doesn't literally mean games, more social interactions and role playing. For example, if a parent says to a frightened child "Don't worry, everything is going to be fine", they can't know it really will be fine. Wittgenstein describes this as a 'words as an instrument of comfort and security' game rather than a 'rational prediction from the available facts' game. Wittgenstein's point is that all kinds of misunderstandings arise when we fail to recognise which kind of game someone is involved in. Another example would be if one's partner says "You never help me. You're so unreliable.". This could be interpreted to be a 'stating the facts' game, like saying "The battle of Waterloo was in 1815". So one might respond by citing facts about how actually you got the car insurance yesterday and you bought some vegetables at lunchtime too. But actually this person is involved in a different language game - they're playing the 'help and reassurance' game, so their "You never help" means "I want you to be more nurturing". Working out the game in question is, Wittgenstein realised, key to good communication. [16]

The autistic brain has great difficulty working out which game is being played. We don't play these games - we stick to stating the facts as that is the logical thing to do.

Paul Dirac (1902 - 1984)

Paul Dirac was a mathematician and theoretical physicist extraordinaire. He accomplished a goal which had eluded all other scientists at the time by combining Einstein's equations of special relativity with those of Schrödinger's quantum mechanics. This required extremely original thought, intense focus and total absorption in his mathematical passion, which in Dirac's case was certainly at the expense of his social skills. Even other scientists thought him extremely antisocial and uncommunicative, but were in total admiration of his 'beautiful' mathematical equations.

All autistic people struggle with social skills, however we can still learn how to get on in the world. I find that people usually respect us for the areas we are good at, particularly in adulthood. Even Dirac, despite his exceptionally poor social skills, was able to rise to the top of his profession, marry and raise a family.

Why is he famous?
Dirac is actually only really famous within the world of physics. Steven Hawking said he was the greatest British theoretical physicist since Newton, yet his achievements far exceed his general fame. He was an early pioneer of the theory of quantum mechanics, and his

book *Principles of Quantum Mechanics* published in 1930 is considered a landmark in the history of science – so much so that it is still in print today nearly 100 years later.

He is particularly famous (amongst physicists) for proposing the 'Dirac equation', which established a connection between relativity and quantum mechanics. This in turn led to another scientific discovery: the prediction of the positron (the antiparticle of the electron, identical to it in every aspect except its charge) and thus the existence of antimatter. As a result, he won the Nobel Prize for physics when he was only 31, which he shared with Erwin Schrödinger. This prediction of antimatter was considered to be the single greatest achievement in twentieth century physics.

Childhood

Dirac was born and brought up in a modest part of Bristol, England. He and his two siblings were raised by their Swiss father and Cornish mother. Life in a bilingual household was difficult for young Dirac; his father worked as a French teacher and was an extremely strict disciplinarian who insisted his children only speak to him in French in order to learn the language. Dirac later recalled very unhappy times as a child when at mealtimes the family was split into two. He would be in the front room having to speak French with his father while his mother and siblings were in the kitchen speaking English. Unable to detach his homelife from his role as a teacher, his father would punish him if he made an error, which resulted in the young Dirac finding it easier to say nothing at all. With little communication between them, his relationship with his father was strained at best. Dirac claimed this to be the origin of his great unwillingness to speak much in later life.

Fortunately, he found reprieve in his studies. His local primary school was supportive and nurturing and set him up well to go on to study at Bristol's highly regarded Merchant Venturers' Technical

College in 1914. Dirac was an outstanding student and began to show an incredible aptitude for maths and physics from a young age. He practically lived in the school library and absorbed all that he could from science books, whilst at home he indulged in comic books and adventure novels.

Adult Life

Dirac was unsure what to study at university, but decided to follow in his brother's footsteps and read engineering at Bristol University. He found the subject easy (and boring), but his curiosity was sparked in November 1919 by news of a remarkable solar eclipse experiment on a small island off the west coast of Africa. The experiment proved that a new theory from an unknown German physicist had been shown to be superior to Newton's famous law of universal gravitation. Almost overnight the name Albert Einstein became known worldwide and Dirac was fascinated by this – he had found his calling. Even though he was an engineering student and theoretical physics was a relatively new subject, Dirac realised that you could sit at your desk and, with a combination of maths and experimental results, come up with the fundamental laws that underlie the fabric of the universe. While other students his age were consumed by thoughts of dating and socialising, Dirac was thinking about mathematical equations and desperately wanting to find out more about this new theory of relativity.

In 1921, he graduated with a first class honours degree, but due to the post-war economic depression, the man who would become a future Nobel prize winner was unable to find a job. Fortunately, a teacher at the university who recognised his outstanding skills in mathematics said he could do a degree in mathematics in only two years, free of charge; it was here that he began to indulge in his obsessive interest in general relativity and quantum mechanics.

Dirac fell in love with what he described as 'beautiful' mathematics – the kind of mathematics that was extremely elegant and concise with an aesthetic appeal all of its own. Producing 'beautiful' mathematical equations is no mean feat, it takes an extraordinary brain to juggle mathematical concepts in your head until exquisite patterns emerge. On top of this, he was also doing applied calculations that demonstrated that this approach was not solely theoretical – it could also be used to understand the physical world. Dirac was proving himself to be both a novel thinker and outstanding mathematician.

Behind the scenes, his father was trying to get his son into the best physics and maths department in the country: Cambridge University. Using his forceful nature for good in this instance, Dirac's father managed to persuade Cambridge that his son was worthy of a scholarship and with that, Dirac began his career as a theoretical physicist in 1923. Dirac was now in an environment where he could truly excel. Cambridge college life provided him with a regular routine and all his daily living needs were met. It suited him perfectly; fellow Cambridge-goers were like-minded people and there was no pressure to socialise.

It didn't take him long to demonstrate his exceptional abilities – he produced six papers within two years, one of which, *The Fundamental Equations of Quantum Mechanics*, still reads like a modern paper. He went on to do a PhD and in June 1926 he submitted his thesis on quantum mechanics which was truly sensational.

That summer, Dirac stayed at the college, working through the holidays rather than going home to Bristol, and wrote another paper on the behaviour of large numbers of electrons. These laws are still used today throughout the world and are fundamental to the development of microelectronics.

Following this project he went to Copenhagen University to work with Niels Bohr, the Danish Nobel Prize winning physicist. This sparked even more original ideas in Dirac's remarkable mind. He wrote yet another great paper here which enabled the different versions of quantum mechanics to be related to one another – a classic paper he called 'My darling' – and four weeks later was the first person to apply quantum theory to electric and magnetic fields.

In February 1927, he moved to Göttingen University in Germany (often referred to as the birthplace of quantum theory), where he worked closely with Robert Oppenheimer and Max Born. Dirac was focused on the monumental task of making regular quantum theory consistent with Einstein's special theory of relativity and later in the year he came up with an equation which brought the two theories together and gave a comprehensive description of the electron. This was 'beautiful' mathematics at its absolute best. Not only did it achieve his goal of combining the two theories, it also explained why the electron has spin, a new property that had never been understood before then, as well as why it had a certain magnetism. The 'Dirac equation', as it subsequently became known, describes the behaviour of electrons and is one of the great triumphs of physics in the twentieth century.

This was a phenomenal time for him and many thought he had reached the pinnacle of his career, but there was more. In 1931, he had another major triumph; he used mathematics, rather than experimentation, to deduce that a particle should exist that had exactly the same mass as an electron but opposite electrical charge. In those days, predicting the existence of particles was unheard of and so his prediction was totally ignored. However, in August 1932 the first track of the anti-electron, or positron, was actually observed. An experimenter called Carl Anderson initially thought his findings were wrong and he didn't even know about Dirac's paper, but on publishing his findings it was recognised to be the first example of antimatter. This discovery earned Dirac a share of the 1933 Nobel Prize for physics and he became the youngest theoretician to win that prize aged just 31.

It's interesting to compare Dirac to Einstein, who used his intense curiosity and extraordinary visual thinking ability to imagine a thought experiment and then went on to work out the maths and equations that explained it. Dirac, on the other hand, thought that maths alone could take you by the hand and lead you into productive pastures for research. This was a new approach to physics and a great example of how the autistic way of thinking can come up with a completely new way of doing something. A lot of modern theoretical physics now follows Dirac's approach.

Dirac was known by his colleagues for his extraordinary intellect, but also for his unusual behaviour. Even Einstein wrote in a letter to Paul Ehrenfest that he thought Dirac was on the border of genius and madness, and Niels Bohr would relate stories about Dirac's eccentricity. On a visit to an art gallery in Copenhagen, for example, they both looked at a French impressionist painting showing a boat sketched by just a few lines and Dirac observed, "This boat looks as if it was not finished". Looking at another picture, Dirac remarked, "I like that because the degree of inaccuracy is the same all over".[1]

Dirac's monosyllabic language and literal-mindedness led to his physicist colleagues competing with one another (in good humour) to see who could tell the most entertaining stories about his bizarre behaviour. His abilities were so highly respected that his minimal social skills were not only tolerated, but fondly relished by his peers.

In 1934, he was introduced to Margit Wigner, the sister of a colleague. She was the polar opposite of him – no scientific background, talked non-stop and made friends easily – yet she was fascinated by him. She would write him an eight-page letter every three days and he would respond every three weeks with a four line letter. Despite this, she persevered and in 1936 they married and went on to have two children. She was very understanding of Dirac, which allowed him to get on with his research while she took charge of everything else. According to his colleagues. marriage changed him: "It's fun to see Dirac married, it makes him so much more human".[2]

In 1971, he took up a professorship at the Florida State University where he published an incredible 60 papers before his death in 1984 – quite the impressive average at five papers a year.

Epitaph
Despite the fact that few people have ever heard of Dirac, his 'beautiful' equation is engraved into the stone floor in Westminster Abbey in front of Newton's tomb – a validation of just how revolutionary and outstanding his work was.

Autistic traits

Special interest
Dirac had a love of mathematics and a desire to explore the mysteries of fundamental physics through beautiful, concise mathematical equations. He was so absorbed in this passion, that he devoted 100% of his brainpower to it, leaving no room for other, more trivial pursuits such as socialising.

Incredible focus
He was extremely obsessive in his approach and once he had set a goal he would not let anything distract him from it. Throughout his whole life he produced a phenomenal amount of work due to this prodigious focus and dedication.

During his postgraduate years, he would spend all his time on his research, except for Sundays when he would take long walks in the countryside; he would scarcely see another person on these walks, which suited him perfectly as he liked to be alone and at one with nature. Walking was a way to put himself in a different environment where he was free to allow his mind to mull over his thoughts and explore new ideas. Even the greatest minds need some downtime.

Abstract thought

Dirac came up with his revolutionary theories and equations purely through thought. He could take the most abstract piece of mathematics and link it all the way through to predictions about the fundamentals of nature. This approach to theoretical physics was phenomenal – all conjured up in his head with no experimental clues, or thought experiments. His breakthrough idea was that the fundamental building blocks of the natural world were based on deep mathematical structures and that finding those mathematical structures will tell us what nature is. Therefore, if he pursued 'beautiful' mathematics it would take him into areas of interest, as indeed it did – in 1927 he successfully predicted the existence of new subatomic particles solely utilising mathematical arguments.

Uneven profile

He was brilliant in his area of interest and expertise at the expense of social skills. A colleague described Dirac as "of towering magnitude in one field, but with little interest and competence left for other human activities".[3] He was so preoccupied with his mathematics that he won a Nobel prize before turning his attention elsewhere. Who else gets a Nobel prize before they get a girlfriend?

Logical thinker

He proposed antimatter not on the basis of physical observation, but purely because his own mathematical logic told him that it must exist. Neils Bohr described Dirac as "a complete logical genius".[4]

Whilst Freeman Dyson said "He seemed to be able to conjure up laws of nature from pure thought".[5]

Literal thinker

After presenting a lecture, a colleague said "I don't understand the equation on the top right hand corner of the blackboard". After a long silence, Dirac was asked if he wanted to answer the question, to which Dirac replied: "That was not a question, it was a comment".[6]

Precise and to the point

Postcards Dirac sent home from college did little more than confirm he was still alive. On a five month rail journey across North America, he kept a diary of his trip in terms of numbers, not words – he didn't write any descriptions of his experiences, just a cumulative record of the number of nights he had spent on a train and on board a ship.

Poor language and communication skills

Asked to explain his discoveries in quantum mechanics, and their significance, Dirac responded that quantum theories are built up "from physical concepts which cannot be explained in words at all".[7]

Niels Bohr once said to Ernest Rutherford, "This Dirac, he seems to know a lot of physics, but he never says anything".[8]

Yet despite his near silence, Dirac quickly earned the enthusiastic friendship and admiration of fellow physicists such as Bohr, Oppenheimer and Heisenberg without, apparently, ever initiating reciprocal entertainment or conversation.

Poor social skills

At college, he came across as being disinterested and rude to his peers and was said to greet every question posed to him with a stark 'yes', 'no', or a blank silence. In fact, his fellow students at St John's, Cambridge, proposed a unit of measurement for the smallest imaginable number of words that a person might utter in conversation, christening the minimum rate of one word per hour as one 'Dirac'.

On the rare occasions when he was provoked into saying more than 'yes' or 'no', he said precisely what he thought, apparently with no understanding of other people's feelings or the conventions of polite conversation. When asked once what he was doing for his holidays, after a long pause he said "Why would you want to know that?". [9]

No interest in small talk

Dirac's manner at the dinner table became the stuff of legend. He had no interest in small talk and it was common for him to sit through several courses without saying a word, or even acknowledging the students sitting next to him. Dirac once responded to the comment "It's a bit rainy, isn't it?" by walking to the window, returning to his seat, and then stating "It is not now raining". [10]

Unbound by social norms

He was completely unconcerned about what other people might think about his eccentric behaviour. For instance, he used to relax by climbing trees in his three-piece suit. It's not that he didn't care what others thought of him, he most likely wasn't aware in the first place this is something most people don't do.

However, perhaps one should step back for a moment and think about this. If you want to climb a tree in a suit, why shouldn't you? For neurotypicals, normal behaviour is what everyone else is doing – they take their cues on how to behave from the people around them in order to fit in. In other words, their behaviour is constrained by the 'box' of social norms. They are unable to behave how they want to as individuals. Their desire to fit in is stronger than their desire to be individual. This is one of the key reasons autistic people are able to think 'outside of the box'.

He also spared no thought as to what he looked like and how he dressed, wearing cheap, unstylish suits whatever the weather until they were threadbare.

Dislike of change
On a trip to the theatre in Germany, Dirac pointedly refused to follow the German practice of leaving headwear in the theatre cloakroom, insisting he took his hat with him to the performance. Being English, Dirac was brought up with English customs and saw no reason to deviate from them in other countries.

Hypersensitive to sudden sounds
Dirac took great care to ensure that he would not be disturbed by chiming bells, or by the sudden barks of neighbourhood dogs. Dogs were permanently banned from his household.

Loyalty
Dirac was known to be extremely loyal to other physicists. Although he had no interest in politics, he campaigned to free his colleague Kapitza from his detention in the Soviet Union and he supported Heisenberg who was shunned by many of his former colleagues for his work on the atom bomb during the war.

What has Paul Dirac done for us?
If it weren't for Dirac, our understanding of fundamental particles simply wouldn't be where it is today. He produced the most comprehensive description of the electron, paving the way for multi-billion pound experiments such as the Large Hadron Collider.

Every aspect of modern technology can be traced back to the extraordinary thinking of theoretical physicists. Dirac's work underpins all of modern physics, and yet is almost impossible to explain to anyone without a good understanding of mathematics and mathematical structures. We therefore have to rely on what other physicists said about him. For instance, his work on matter and antimatter was described by Heisenberg as "the biggest of all big jumps in twentieth-century physics".[11]

George Orwell (1903 - 1950)

A common thread amongst many of the characters in this book is their ability to boil down complex ideas into simple terms and Orwell was no exception. He was able to make the extraordinarily complicated world of politics more accessible to the public by writing books, which used down-to-earth stories and straightforward metaphors that anyone could understand.

In a similar vein, one of my main objectives in my talks and books is to make the complicated world of autism more accessible – many people are 'aware' of autism to the same extent they are aware of quantum mechanics! Autism is a hugely complex subject, not only because it's an invisible condition, but also because it affects people in very different ways. I explain what we have in common, whilst bringing our positive attributes to light.

Why is he famous?

George Orwell is considered to be the most significant British political writer of the twentieth century. He is famous for his novels *Animal Farm* and *Nineteen Eighty-Four*, which are two of the most studied novels in English literature due to their unique perspective and original views of human nature. By 2007, they had sold almost

50 million copies in 62 languages, more than any other pair of books by a twentieth-century author. In 2017, *Nineteen Eighty-Four* reached the top of the US Amazon's best sellers list, an affirmation of the appeal and relevance Orwell's writing still commands today. He was a master at writing allegories – stories that can be interpreted to reveal a hidden meaning, typically a moral or political one.

His books have made such an impact that the word 'Orwellian' is now in the English dictionary and is used to describe totalitarian or authoritarian practices. Other words and concepts he introduced, for example 'Big Brother' and 'Room 101', are also in common use today.

Childhood

George Orwell, born 'Eric Arthur Blair', started out life in Bengal, India, where his father worked for the British government in the civil service. In 1904, his mother took the then one-year-old Orwell and his six-year-old sister back to England to be raised and educated – a common occurrence amongst English colonial families at the time. Although he only spent the first year of his life in Bengal, this exposure to a world beyond England inadvertently gave him a taste of adventure that was to define his entire life.

Reminiscing on his childhood as an adult, Orwell described it as a "somewhat lonely" experience; he was the middle child of three with a gap of five years on either side and he rarely saw his father due to his demanding role overseas.[1] To keep himself entertained, young Orwell would make up stories and was often caught holding conversations with imaginary friends. Aside from the figments of his imagination, animals were his closest confidants – from dogs and cats to rabbits and guinea pigs, he was deeply devoted to the family's many pets.

Perhaps it was out of this childhood solitude that his creativity was born. Orwell was a bright child and at the age of eight, he was sent to a prestigious boarding school, St Cyprian's, in the seaside town of Eastbourne in Sussex. The school primarily catered for children from wealthy families, preparing them to gain a place in the likes of Harrow or Eton, but Orwell won a scholarship to attend and it was here that he first experienced class politics. Pupils were treated differently depending on their background and despite his age, it didn't take Orwell long to pick up on how unfair this was. Such politics would later become a defining feature of his writing.

He disliked his time at St Cyprian's for a whole host of reasons – the primary one being that bullying was rife. Not only was Orwell an avid reader, but a thoughtful, sensitive and mature young boy, qualities which immediately marked him apart from the other boys. The gang of bullies would mock and harass the pupils they perceived as swots, so Orwell was an obvious target. Even the headmaster's wife was a bully. She would pull the boys' hair to make them 'learn', but Orwell was quick-witted and soon figured out how to avoid her heavy hands; he would grease his hair so that her fingers were unable to gain any grip.

The food at the school was equally awful. He recalled the porridge as containing "more lumps, hairs and unexplained black things than one would have thought possible, unless someone were putting them there on purpose".[2] And yet what Orwell disliked the most was the style of teaching. He described the education process as "cramming him with large doses of information that was either useless or wrong".[3] In his history lessons, he felt that they were encouraged to learn dates, without "the faintest interest in the meaning of the mysterious events they were naming".[4] This textbook-led teaching left Orwell's natural thirst for knowledge and truth completely unsatisfied.

Orwell's way with words was evident from a young age and whilst still only a schoolchild, he had two poems published in the local newspaper. In 1917, he won a scholarship to Eton, where he quickly honed his literary skills by getting involved in producing the college magazine and other publications. But whilst having fun crafting an early writing career during extracurricular activities, his academic studies fell to the wayside. His parents couldn't afford to send him to a university without another scholarship and from his poor results, it was clear that he wouldn't be able to win one.

Adult Life

With no university prospects after his stint at Eton, Orwell made his way to Burma and joined the Indian Imperial Police Force. Whilst there, he served in a number of country stations, but when he saw how much the Burmese were ruled by the British against their will, he felt increasingly uncomfortable as a colonial police officer.

Five years later, he returned to England with a deep hatred for imperialism – a fairly radical stance for him to take given his upbringing. Determined to take his life in a new direction and fulfil his ambition to be a writer, he made his way to Paris where he started work on his first novel (that no one would publish and which he later destroyed). His money soon ran out and he ended up working as a dishwasher in a hotel. Life was hard and he lived mostly from hand to mouth, going hungry on several occasions; but having witnessed the intricacies of class politics both in England and abroad, Orwell actually wanted to experience what it was like to be poor in order to be able to truthfully write about the struggles of the lower classes.

After a period of time in Paris, he returned to London where he lived for months amongst the labourers and beggars in the East End to further his first-hand knowledge of poverty and their way of life. His first book *Down and Out in Paris and London*, published in 1933, drew on these experiences and it was from then that he started using the pen name George Orwell, because he didn't want his family to suffer any embarrassment from the book. George came from the reigning King George V and Orwell from the local river.

In 1936, Orwell was commissioned by Victor Gollancz, a socially conscious publisher, to write about mass unemployment in Lancashire and Yorkshire. Gollancz thought that if only people could be made to know the nature of poverty, they would want to eradicate it, remove the government that tolerated it and transform the economic system that brought it into being.

Thrilled to have been invited to expose class division, a topic very close to his heart, Orwell enthusiastically took on this project and his powerful description of the poverty he witnessed there resulted in the book *The Road to Wigan Pier*. With two successful books published, he could now live on his earnings from writing and so moved to the small countryside village of Wallington in Hertfordshire. Ready to establish a base after years on the move, he married Eilleen O'Shaughnessy, an Oxford graduate and trained psychologist that he had met in Hampstead a year earlier.

But Orwell was restless and still felt that there was work to be done. In order to establish a more accurate perspective of politics and the class problem, he decided to go to Spain to join the civil war in the fight against facism – saying, "It was the first time where I'd been in a town where the working class were in the saddle".[5] He joined the militia, but ended up getting shot and, weakened by tuberculosis, took over a year to recover in a sanatorium. Having gone through such an ordeal, he was lucky to get out of Spain alive. This was a turning point in his life and thereafter all work, directly or indirectly, was written as a protest to highlight the injustices of totalitarianism.

The idea of *Animal Farm* came to him when he saw a small boy of about 10 years old driving a huge carthorse along a narrow path and whipping it every time it tried to turn. It occurred to him that men exploit animals in much the same way that the rich exploit the working classes. The story is an allegory about communist rule in the Soviet Union, which Orwell was very much against, and almost every detail has political significance. He said *Animal Farm* was the first book "in which I tried with full consciousness of what I was doing, to fuse political purpose and artistic purpose into one realm. What I most wanted was to turn political writing into an art".[6]

The book was divisive to say the least. It was initially rejected by publishers, one of which decided to consult the Ministry of Information, who strongly advised him against publishing it because it was thought too controversial at a time in which the Soviet Union was a powerful ally of Britain against Germany. This was despite the fact that Stalin's totalitarian government had been widely condemned for overseeing mass repression, ethnic cleansing, wide-scale deportation, hundreds of thousands of executions and famines that killed millions. Another publisher objected to the choice of pigs as the protagonists of the story, worried that such portrayal would offend Russian readers.

Animal Farm was finally published in 1945 on the brink of the Cold War – the tense period of rivalry that developed after World War II between the United States and the Soviet Union (and their respective allies). The Cold War was waged on political, economic and propaganda fronts. Interestingly, Orwell himself coined the term 'Cold War' in an article published the same year to refer to what he predicted would be a nuclear stalemate between "two or three monstrous super-states, each possessed of a weapon by which millions of people can be wiped out in a few seconds".[7] The timing of *Animal Farm*'s anti-Soviet message was perfect and led to it becoming a critical triumph and bestseller.

The limelight may have been on *Animal Farm*, but Orwell was already full of ideas for his next piece of fiction, keen to create something far darker and more complex than any of his previous works. In fact, he wanted to write a novel influenced by all the experiences he had gained over his entire life. However, due to the success of *Animal Farm*, he was continually distracted by invitations to lecture, or join societies, when all he wanted was to have the space and time to think. To ensure a clear diary (and a clear head), he moved to the remote Hebridean island of Jura where he could work in peace on his new novel amongst the wild, isolated beauty of the island.

The new book, provisionally entitled *The Last Man in Europe*, drew heavily on Orwell's experiences of propaganda and totalitarianism in the Spanish Civil War. And insights from his time working for the BBC Empire Service during WWII – where he was involved in creating the propaganda fed to Indian networks to encourage a pro-Allies sentiment and spark volunteering – also played a big part in his approach to the novel. Ultimately, the book dealt with the consequences to society of totalitarianism, mass surveillance and authoritarianism, with the story examining the role of truth and facts within politics and the ways in which they are manipulated.

By the end of 1948, the typescript of Orwell's completed novel reached London and his publisher Fred Warburg at once recognised its dystopian qualities describing it as "amongst the most terrifying books I have ever read".[8] The book, renamed *Nineteen Eighty-Four*, was published on 8 June 1949 and was almost universally considered a masterpiece. Today, it remains as fresh and sharply resonant as when it was first published.

Shortly after the famed publication, Orwell's tuberculosis finally caught up with him and he eventually passed away in January 1950.

Autistic traits

Ability to simplify complex subjects
Orwell was appalled by what was happening in Stalinist Russia and realised that what at first glance seemed like a utopian idea that all people should be equal, had quickly degenerated into totalitarianism. He was able to look at the complex, political situation in Russia and boil it down to the obvious fact that human nature is such that some people will always be greedy, selfish and power hungry. Autistic people often have the ability to point out what is sometimes blatantly obvious and Orwell had this ability in spades. He was thus able to capture the essence of what was actually going on, in his simple, almost childlike story about farmyard animals: *Animal Farm*.

Independent thinker
Even as a schoolboy he thought for himself and challenged what he was being taught. Tutors and students alike recall how argumentative he was, always criticising the masters, as well as the other boys. He never wanted to simply accept the information supplied to him; he questioned everything and came up with his own conclusions.

His work was always impartial – he simply wrote his mind regardless of what others would think, reserving some of the most severe criticisms for left-wing authors of the time even though he himself was a left-wing writer.

Attention to detail
He wanted to describe people and situations as accurately as possible and would focus on aspects of things that would normally go unnoticed. To achieve this he found it best to write from experience. In order to write a truthful account of the poor, he went to great lengths to immerse himself in the lives of the working class – from

dressing in tramp's clothing to living with vagrants and those in extreme poverty – in order to expose *exactly* what it was like.

Straightforward use of language
Orwell had a passion for clarity in language and this is one of the defining features of his work. His prose is clear and succinct and it is the precision of his writing style that makes his message even more profound. Autistic people prefer to use straightforward and concise language to avoid ambiguity and misunderstandings and that is precisely how Orwell composed his stories, keeping his prose plain and direct.

Tenacity
Orwell was a workaholic. He worked long and hard – even in ill health – and it was his sheer willpower and dogged determination that led to him achieving his goal to be a successful writer.

An insight into Orwell's passion for his work is revealed in a letter his wife wrote, in which she suggests that their early days of marriage were difficult due to her husband's workaholic tendencies: "I cried all the time.. Partly because Eric had decided that he mustn't let his work be interrupted and complained bitterly when we'd been married a week that he'd only done two good days' work out of seven".[9]

Craving for honesty and truthfulness
During his time in the Spanish Civil War he saw newspaper reports which did not bear any relation to the facts: "I saw great battles reported where there had been no fighting and complete silence where hundreds of men had been killed".[10] He knew that the propaganda reported by papers and on the radio made it impossible to obtain a reliable version of events. This greatly disturbed Orwell, who hated this deception and wanted the facts and the truth about totalitarianism to be reported. The traumatic events of that war

inspired his extremely frank essay entitled *Homage to Catalonia*, which is often described as one of the finest first-hand works about countrymen slaughtering one another.

This distaste for propaganda became one of the key themes of *Nineteen Eighty-Four*. He knew from his time at the BBC that much of what the BBC reported needed prior approval by the Ministry of Information.

Strong sense of justice and fairness

Orwell's strong sense of justice and fairness developed at school. Caning was common, but it was the injustice and arbitrariness of the punishment that really upset him.

His works demonstrate his profound awareness and distaste for social injustice and he was an outspoken supporter of democratic socialism:

> What I have most wanted to do is to make political writing into an art. My starting point is always a feeling of partisanship, a sense of injustice. I write because there is some lie that I want to expose, some fact to which I want to draw attention.[11]

His way of doing this was to write allegorical stories which exposed the evils of totalitarianism.

Logical thinker

One reason he chose the pen name 'Orwell' was because he wanted a name that started with a letter in the middle of the alphabet. This was to make sure his books would be placed on the middle shelf in a bookshop. Not too high, where customers would not see them, and not too low where they would be near their feet.

Poor social skills

Colleagues described Orwell as being shy, brusque and unsociable. A further indication of his poor social skills was his inability to engage in small talk. Conversely, when talking about birds and animals (one of his special interests) he was a mine of information to the point of being a bore.

Awkward appearance and uncoordinated

He was a tall, gangly, badly coordinated man who looked as if he'd grown out of his clothes. A friend described him as "awfully likely to knock things off tables and trip over things. I think his feeling was that even the inanimate world was against him".[12] When working for the BBC in the 1940s, people would make fun of him and saw him as having real entertainment value "like watching a Charlie Chaplin movie".[12]

Love of sameness

Such a fan was he of a classic British cup of tea, that when he was in Spain, Orwell had Fortnum and Mason's tea delivered to him. The shape of the cup was also important to him; it should be cylindrical, not flat and shallow, and he even wrote a guide on how to make the perfect cup entitled *A Nice Cup Of Tea*, which was published in the Evening Standard in 1946.

What has George Orwell done for us?

Orwell's books make people think about how our society functions, encouraging debates and discussions about the future. He was able to simplify political ideology in a way that made it accessible to the general public.

Orwell's *Nineteen Eighty-Four* was written as a warning to mankind about the dangers of a surveillance state and the power of the mass media to manipulate public opinion, history and even the truth.

Even today, *Nineteen Eighty-Four* resonates strongly with people in real life. When Donald Trump, famous for his proclamations of 'fake news' and 'alternative facts', became President of the United States in January 2017, US sales of the book rocketed by almost 10,000% – propelling it to the top of Amazon's best-seller list.

George Orwell gave us a profoundly important message: "The moral to be drawn from this dangerous nightmare situation is a simple one," he said when *Nineteen Eighty-Four* was published, "Don't let it happen. It depends on you".[13]

Alan Turing (1912 - 1954)

Autistic people tend to think very logically and analytically, similar in many ways to how a computer operates. Throughout his life, Alan Turing addressed problems from a very logical and mathematical perspective. I suspect it was this autistic way of thinking that led him to believe that it might be possible to design and build a machine that could not only process complex mathematical problems, but also work like a brain: a machine where programs and files are stored in memory and accessed when required.

How the human brain operated obsessed Turing, but he was also fascinated by subjects such as philosophy, logic, maths and biology; he would draw information from all these sources and search for links between them. In effect, he was a one man 'team' who, instead of approaching a problem from just the maths perspective, would also consider the philosophical and logical angles. It was this 'out of the box' way of thinking that led him to design and create a machine that can be said to have altered the course of human history and to be the start of the technological age we live in today.

Why is he famous?

Turing is remembered primarily for his work during World War II in which he played a crucial role designing and building a code-breaking machine that deciphered encrypted messages from Germany. This provided vital information, which ultimately led to the shortening of the war by an estimated two years, thus saving millions of lives.

Another major achievement was a scientific paper he wrote that outlined the fundamental principles of the modern computer. Although the technology to build such a machine simply did not exist at the time, he effectively invented the concept of software programs that would run on a computer. Every computer and smartphone in use today uses this idea.

He made groundbreaking contributions to the fields of mathematics, biology and chemistry (chemists consider him to be the father of chaos theory). And, as if that wasn't enough, he also proposed the famous 'Turing Test' as a means of determining a machine's ability to exhibit intelligent behaviour equivalent to, or indistinguishable from, that of a human. This then led to the development of artificial intelligence.

Childhood

Alan was taken by numbers even before he could read. As a child, he would often stop at lamp posts and study the serial number, his mother fondly recalled. Conversely, he showed no interest in reading until, at the age of five, he found a book that fascinated him so much that he proceeded to teach himself to read in just three weeks. This was characteristic of a lifelong habit of having no interest whatsoever in being taught things by other people and instead wanting to find everything out for himself in his own way. From a young age, he was determined and independent with a craving for the literal and frank truth.

Alan's father worked for the civil service in India, so he and his elder brother spent most of their childhood in England living with family and friends, or at boarding school, only seeing their parents for holidays. It was during one of these holidays that his parents first really took notice of their son's unusual talents. Nature and science had always enthralled him, but his keen observation of the world around him during one summer in North West Scotland was quite dumbfounding. Aged just seven years old, intrigued by the life of the humble honeybee, he took it upon himself to observe the flight path of nearby bees and then, by plotting the intersection point, directed himself to the hive.

At the age of 13, he was sent to Sherborne School, a boarding school in Dorset. The first day of term coincided with the 1926 General Strike (which meant no trains were running), but Alan was so determined not to miss his first day of school that he rode his bicycle the 60 miles from Southampton. This feat astonished his peers and was even published in the local newspaper.

According to his school report, Turing was an antisocial teenager who more often than not, opted not to mix with his peer group. But this wasn't entirely true, as he did have one good friend who shared his passion for maths and science, as well as his hobbies of origami and cryptography (writing and solving secret coded messages). His lack of eye contact, awkward appearance, serious stutter and high-pitched voice were all attributes that likely didn't help with his social status, yet generally, his peers accepted him for who he was. Despite his eccentricities and his social issues, he reportedly had a great sense of humour – particularly loving pranks and practical jokes – which his fellow students appreciated.

Although he excelled in his areas of interest, he was bottom of the class in English and his handwriting, according to his English teacher, was "the worst she had ever seen".[1] On the other hand, he was exceptionally brilliant for his age at science and maths. At 15, when his grandfather gave him a copy of Einstein's exposition of relativity theory, he became utterly engrossed and even wrote a summary explaining the theory for his mother. Yet he nearly failed most of his exams because he was hopeless at all the other subjects – the headmaster actually wrote to his parents and said he was wasting his time at public school if he was only going to concentrate on the sciences. However, on the last Prize Giving day, the headmaster clearly had a change of heart and recognised that, having at first been something of a misfit in public school life, "Turing in his sphere is one of the most distinguished boys the school has had in recent years".[2]

Adult Life

In 1931, Turing went to King's College, Cambridge, to study mathematics. This was an environment in which he was with like-minded people and could truly thrive – not only intellectually with fellow mathematicians, but also socially by joining sports clubs. He made the College rowing team and enjoyed cycling and skiing holidays with his peers. In 1934, he gained a first-class honours degree in mathematics.

A year later, aged just 22, he was awarded a fellowship at King's as a result of his dissertation in which he proved a long-standing mathematical puzzle (the 'Entscheidungsproblem') – an astonishing feat in mathematics for anyone, let alone a recently qualified graduate. Turing was already on track for a distinguished career in pure mathematics, but he had a passion for finding practical uses for abstract mathematical ideas and this pushed him into the field of mathematical logic.

In 1936, Turing published a truly historic paper which laid the groundwork for the technological age we live in today. The philosophical paper, *On Computable Numbers*, hypothesised a machine that could compute any problem that a human could. He proposed a 'Universal Turing machine' capable of tackling any kind of problem by storing instructional code in the computer's memory. Turing's ideas about memory storage and using a single machine to carry out all tasks laid the foundation for what would become the modern computer.

At the outbreak of the Second World War, Turing was recruited (together with other promising mathematicians) to work at Bletchley Park, Britain's secret code-breaking centre. Turing immediately got to work designing a code-breaking machine, the Bombe – so called because of the relentless ticking sound that the machine made, leading operators to remark that it sounded like a time bomb waiting to go off. The Bombe shortened the steps required in decoding and 200 of them were built for British use over the course of the war. The groundbreaking machine allowed codebreakers to decipher up to 4,000 messages a day.

His next great achievement was cracking the Enigma, a mechanical device used by the German army to encode secure messages. Due to the millions of computations involved, it was almost impossible to decrypt without the correct cipher, which the Germans changed every day. Eventually breaking the code enabled the interception of the German naval communications about the German U-boat attacks on the allied ships carrying vital supplies across the Atlantic.

Early on, Bletchley Park's operations were hampered by a lack of resources, but pleas for better staffing were ignored by government officials. So, Turing went over their heads to write directly to Prime Minister Winston Churchill and one of his fellow codebreakers hand delivered the letter in October 1941. In response, Churchill immediately ordered his chief of staff to "Make sure they have all they want on extreme priority and report to me that this had been done".[3]

Anyone who's watched the film *The Imitation Game* about Turing's work at Bletchley Park might conclude that he had no sense of humour, or little interest in the joys of life. In reality, this couldn't be further from the truth. Despite being uncompromisingly unconventional, he relished socialising and liked to go out drinking and dancing with his colleagues, who described him as warm and funny, with a mischievous and infectious sense of humour. He had a girlfriend at Bletchley and would often take her to the cinema, or dancing. It's clear, therefore, that he got on with likeminded people – I imagine most of his peers at Bletchley would also have displayed many autistic characteristics and my experience of attending CASPA, a local youth club for autistic kids, tells me that autistic people can enjoy socialising with each other immensely.

At the end of World War II, Turing was awarded an OBE for his services to his country, which – to the amusement of his friends – he kept in a tin box along with a collection of screws, nails, nuts and bolts.

In 1945, while working at the UK's National Physical Laboratory, he invented the Automatic Computing Machine, the first digital computer with stored programs. This was yet another major accomplishment – previous computers didn't have electric memory storage and had to be manually rewired to switch between different programs.

In 1950, he published another astonishing paper entitled *Computing Machinery and Intelligence*, which was to become a key contributor to the field of artificial intelligence. In it, Turing suggested 'the imitation game' as a way to assess how successfully a machine can mimic human behaviour. He proposed that whether or not a computer can convince a person that it is human would be the best measure of artificial intelligence. This later became known as the famous 'Turing Test'.

A year later, Turing turned his attention to computational biology and published another seminal paper *The Chemical Basis of Morphogenesis*, which dealt with the development of patterns and shapes in biological organisms. This triggered a whole new field of mathematical enquiry into pattern formation.

On the evening of 6 June 1954, Turing had been gold-plating spoons in his spare room, a process that uses potassium cyanide. The next morning, his housekeeper found that he had died in his sleep. Various conspiracy theories have grown up around this, mainly relating to his secret war work; but his death was probably accidental due to the inhalation of cyanide gas produced during the electroplating process.

For many years after his death, his major contributions to the war effort were unknown, because his work was classified top secret and only became public in the 1970s. This work, in combination with his other achievements, is now celebrated – the prestigious Turing Award is the equivalent of a Nobel prize for achievement in the field of computer science.

Autistic traits

Out of the box thinking
Turing's special interests comprised a range of disciplines including maths, logic, chemistry, biology and philosophy. I think Turing's out of the box thinking was largely a result of drawing from this range of subjects and seeing connections and links between them, rather than approaching things from one frame of reference. For example, his interest in how the brain works, combined with his maths and logic

expertise, led to the development of a computer that works 'like a brain', as well as to his innovations in the field of artificial intelligence.

Insatiable curiosity and thirst for knowledge

When he was 10 years old he was given a copy of *Natural Wonders Every Child Should Know* by Edwin Tenney Brewster, which he read from cover to cover and this made a big impression on him, opening his eyes to the world of science. One chapter was about the nature of the mind and the brain which particularly fascinated him and led to his all-absorbing and lifelong interest in the subject.

Focus

He was extremely focused and would often work through the night when he was stuck on a particular problem. As a child, he was described by his brother as being a highly disciplined character capable of becoming an expert in pretty much anything he had an interest in. I see this slightly differently – who needs to be self-disciplined when the subject is just so interesting that you can't tear yourself away from it, like reading a book that you can't put down?

Turing also displayed a passion and focus for long distance running. He would go for a run every day (he said it helped him think) and would sometimes run to scientific meetings and actually beat his colleagues who travelled by public transport. He regularly ran the 31 miles between Cambridge and Ely when he was at King's College and he occasionally ran the 40 miles between London and Bletchley Park.

He was a member of the Walton Athletics Club and, quite remarkably, was a world-class marathon runner, coming fifth in the trials for the 1948 Olympics. One member remembers him joining the club:

We heard him rather than saw him. He made a terrible grunting noise when he was running, but before we could say anything to him, he was past us like a shot out of a gun. A couple of nights later, we kept up with him long enough for me to ask him who he ran for. When he said nobody, we invited him to join Walton. He did and immediately became our best runner. I asked him one day why he punished himself so much in training. He told me "I have such a stressful job that the only way I can get it out of my mind is by running hard; it's the only way I can get some release".[4]

Pattern recognition

Spotting patterns is essential for code breaking and deciphering and was a skill at which Turing was truly a master. The Enigma machine had 159 quintillion (a million million million) possibilities – too many to process in 24 hours before the settings were changed again. Therefore, the only possible solution was to find a pattern in the messages sent, which could be used as a shortcut. The breakthrough came when they realised that a weather report was the first message sent each day; spotting this pattern dramatically reduced the number of possibilities and ultimately led to them cracking the code.

Uneven profile

At school, he excelled at the subjects he was interested in, which were all related to science and nature, but he was bottom of the class in English. This demonstrates a typically autistic uneven profile (which I too displayed at school) and teachers often find it hard to understand that a pupil can be exceptionally good at certain subjects and absolutely hopeless at others. They think we're lazy and not trying, but it's usually because we have no interest in some subjects and simply don't see the point in studying them.

Dislike for small talk

Turing described social chat as "vapid conversation" and simply couldn't stand it.[5] When his brother invited him to a sherry party at his house, Turing arrived nearly an hour late, looking dishevelled and left within ten minutes without a word of apology, or excuse. Throughout his life, Turing was extremely economical with his words unless it was to do with one of his interests. He carried out a huge correspondence with other mathematicians all over the world yet rarely wrote to his relatives; before visiting them, for example, he would simply send a telegram stating "arriving today" with no other details.[6]

Non-conformity

Turing was a non-conformer in the truest sense of the word – he actually enjoyed being non-conformist, once saying "I had a very agreeable sense of irresponsibility, rather like being back at school".[7] As a pupil he was determined to do things his own way. Some teachers thought he was both lazy and insolent, but what annoyed them most was his tendency to pay no attention at all during lessons, then cram for exams at the last minute and score high marks. He positively enjoyed beating the system and refused to work at anything except his precious maths and science. At Sherborne, marks were awarded both for course work and examination results and on one occasion he was twenty-second out of twenty-three on the term's work, but first in exams.

Eccentric behaviour

I'm not sure whether eccentric behaviour is just another manifestation of non-conformity, but Turing certainly had a reputation for eccentricity. At Bletchley Park, his colleagues remembered him chaining his tea mug to the radiator to ensure that it was never stolen or removed. Sometimes, he appeared in the office in his pyjamas, or wore trousers held up by a striped necktie instead of a belt. His hair was unkempt and he had a permanent 'five o'clock shadow', refusing to shave with anything but an ancient electric razor.

He would even arrive at conferences at the Foreign Office in London having run the 40 miles from Bletchley in old trousers and a vest – on one occasion with an alarm clock tied around his waist, because his watch had gone wrong. He was also known for wearing a gas mask when cycling in the area around Bletchley because he suffered from acute hay fever and the mask gave him some protection from the pollen. He was completely indifferent to the fact that other people might see his behaviour as ridiculous, even alarming. Turing determinedly always took the logical approach rather than the conventional one.

Awkward appearance

Turing was friends with the mathematician Max Newman and his wife Lyn. She recalled "his oddly-contoured head", his "almost shambling" gait and that he never looked right in his clothes; whether it was a well-worn jacket that looked a size too small, or when he took pains to wear a smart white shirt and his best tweed suit.[8] He also "had a strange way of not meeting the eye, of sidling out of the door with a brusque and off-hand word of thanks".[9]

Irreverence

Turing was impatient with officialdom of any kind, found it hard to defer to his superiors and lacked the respect for authority that society expects. A classic example of this being in 1941 when he went over his boss's heads and wrote directly to Winston Churchill to ask for more funds for the code-breaking programme. I find it refreshing that the Prime Minister listened to Turing, as the country's leading expert in the field. He understood that Turing's team could give Britain a competitive edge in the war.

Conversely, he was keen to share his knowledge with anyone who showed an interest, regardless of their status – for example, he gave two scientific talks to a group of women at the Adult School in Guildford with no suggestion of condescension. He always accepted people on their personal merits, irrespective of their background.

Literal thinking

Like myself, he had a tendency to take things literally. An entertaining example of this was when he didn't sign his identity card during the war because of the explicit instruction 'Do not write on this card'.

Another example was his response to the 'Entscheidungsproblem' in his historic 1936 paper. Turing's approach took the problem literally. One of his teachers, Max Newman, had formulated the problem as the possibility of finding a mechanical process for deciding whether a proposition or its opposite was formally provable. Turing took the phrase 'mechanical process' absolutely literally by defining a machine and the way it works so that what that machine is doing is mathematics.

It's important to note that in 1936 'computers' meant 'one who computes'; in other words, a person performing mathematical calculations (the first recorded use of the term 'computer' actually dates from 1613). Turing shows brilliantly in the paper that whatever a human computer can do, a machine can.

What has Alan Turing done for us?

The revolutionary thing that Turing did for us has to be his contribution to the invention of the computer (you probably have a Universal Turing Machine in your pocket right now – your smartphone). Indeed, all of the computers on the planet can trace their technology directly back to Alan Turing's revolutionary 1936 paper, *On Computable Numbers*.

His work on artificial intelligence also has a major impact on our lives today. The huge advances in computer power and enormous increase in the volume of data being produced every day have opened the doors for artificial intelligence to enable many new technologies – think self-driving cars, medical diagnoses from images, facial recognition and even music and film recommendations. It's literally transforming the world we live in.

However, his most famous contribution to the world must be his phenomenal code-breaking skills which, during the Second World War, without doubt helped to save millions of lives.

Andy Warhol (1928 - 1987)

Autistic people often think very visually and find that they are better able to understand the world and convey information through pictures rather than through the complexities of the English language.

Andy Warhol falls into this category. Using images of popular American culture, he produced a completely original form of art that visualised his ideas about consumerism and fame in a way that was far more powerful than words could possibly convey. It is difficult to overstate what a huge impact he made on the art world, both by redefining what art is and by making it accessible to everyone (not just 'fine art' aficionados), hence the invention of a completely new term to reflect this: Popular Art or 'Pop Art'.

I'm able to relate to his thought processes, because my autistic brain also likes to visualise concepts. To understand idioms when I was young, for example, I would visualise the literal meaning, draw the image that came into my head and write the true meaning below. My simple line drawings give an insight into how autistic people process language and can be seen as pieces of art in their own right. Some of these pictures can be found on display in a gallery at Bromley College.

Why is he famous?

Revolutionary, eccentric and prolific, Warhol produced some of the most famous, valuable and controversial works of art ever made. In my opinion, he is up there with Picasso as one of the most original, far sighted and influential artists of the twentieth century. He was instrumental in the creation of the Pop Art movement, which introduced modern art to the general public.

Warhol was a master at creating iconic images; his silkscreen prints of celebrities, such as Marilyn Monroe, and popular consumer goods, like Coca Cola bottles, being perfect examples. His work was criticised at the time as being lightweight and vacuous, which is ironic as in fact his work reflected these very aspects of American consumerism and obsession with celebrity.

His work is some of the most sought after and valuable art in the world – as iconic today as when first created. In 2008, *Eight Elvises* resold for an immense $100 million, making it one of the most expensive paintings ever sold.

Childhood

Just over a year before the Great Crash of 1929, Andrew Warhola – better known as 'Andy Warhol' – was born to Eastern European parents in the industrial city of Pittsburgh, Pennsylvania. Warhol's beginnings were definitively working class and his formative years shaped by the hardships of the Great Depression, which lasted until 1939; his father was a construction worker and his mother was an embroiderer. They worked hard to support Andy and his two older brothers in a time when the 'American Dream' had become more like an American nightmare. But despite their struggles, Warhol was brought up in a loving environment by parents who nurtured his creative intelligence from a young age.

Even as a child, his appearance was what most people would consider unusual. He was a small, thin boy with a pallid complexion caused by the various ailments that he suffered from in childhood. His distinctive pale skin and stark white hair (which became his trademark as an adult), made him stand out from the crowd from early on.

Warhol was a sickly child and contracted rheumatic fever when he was eight years old. The disease of the nervous system was fairly common in children at the time and resulted in him being confined to bed for a few months. Keen to keep him occupied, his skilled and artistic mother used this time to engage her youngest son in his first drawing lessons, which was soon to become Warhol's favourite childhood hobby. Whether drawing, making collages, watching films, or listening to music, he whiled away his hours spent in confinement through the many mediums of art. Warhol later described this period as a pivotal point in his development as an artist.

When not drawing, he was engrossed in the latest comics, with Popeye and Dick Tracy being particular favourites, and he found great comfort in the company of Tom and Jerry and Mickey Mouse cartoons. But it was Hollywood that marked Warhol's deepest obsession. Perhaps due to how starkly different this world was from his own, he became a complete Hollywood movie fanatic and would go to the movies as often as finances allowed – absorbing the glitzy culture and completely taken with the allure of the beautiful people and the fantasy worlds they inhabited. Desperate to have a little bit of Hollywood for himself, he persuaded his brother to write to the studios and ask the movie stars to send him a signed photograph of themselves, which many of them did. His scrapbook of autographed photographs was his prized possession.

At the age of nine, his mother treated him to his very own camera and photography soon became another of his passions. He even set up a makeshift dark room in the basement, so that he could develop his own photographs.

His mother may have sparked his passion, but Warhol's artistic tendencies came into their own at Schenley High School. The particularly good art department came complete with an enthusiastic art teacher, so it was here that he spent most of his time. He was a quiet and exceptionally shy student, but never failed to impress with his disciplined and self-directed approach to work. Warhol's talents were quickly recognised by his teachers and attracted the attention of the other students, who often huddled around his desk to watch him draw. His most beloved possession was his sketchbook, which went everywhere with him, allowing him to draw at every opportunity.

After leaving school in 1945, he went on to study commercial art at the Carnegie Institute of Technology. Never one to think *inside* the box, Warhol didn't make it to the end of first year without intervention – when his unconventional ideas and ways of producing art didn't quite match the standard of the art course, he was suspended and told to attend summer school to get back on course. But Warhol's talent was of course undeniable and once he grasped what was expected of him, he was able to graduate with a Bachelor of Fine Art in pictorial design.

Adult Life
Aged 21, Warhol made the move to the 'Big Apple' to pursue a career as a commercial artist. New York may have been daunting and Warhol may have been painfully shy, but that didn't stop him

securing his first professional hire within 48 hours of arriving in the city. By simply walking into the offices of Glamour Magazine and asking to see the editor, Warhol's direct approach quickly paid off. The magazine's editor, Tina Fredricks, entertained the brazen young artist and was quickly won over when Warhol presented his portfolio, which spoke for itself – she loved his novel illustrations of butterflies and cakes and immediately hired him to illustrate an article.

And Tina Fredricks wasn't the only one to be impressed by Warhol's prodigious talent and quirky personality. Although now a young man, Warhol retained a childlike quality that endeared him to people, so his success was swift. He was soon doing assignments for all the prestigious glossy magazines, from Vogue to Harper's Bazaar, as well as for top New York department stores. Throughout the 1950s, he worked relentlessly and produced an enormous output of illustrations for fashion advertisements, books, record albums and many other promotional items. This determined approach to his work saw him win numerous accolades, including designer and artist of the year. Warhol was *the* illustrator in New York.

Having established himself as a successful commercial artist, his next goal was to become an artist in his own right, by composing and producing his own art on his own terms.

A little over a decade after he had first landed in New York, in the summer of 1962, Warhol held his first major exhibition at the Ferus Gallery in Los Angeles. Still universally recognised today, the exhibition featured a set of 32 Campbell soup can paintings (one of each of the available varieties), which he hung around the gallery to resemble a grocery store. The exhibition caused a sensation, as it challenged the public's preconceptions about art – up to that point consumer goods like soup cans were considered trivial, even improper subject matter for serious art. Most artists don't produce their greatest, most iconic work until much later in their careers, but

Warhol's first solo show was so radical that it's still regarded as his most legendary work.

A year later, he converted a former warehouse space to use as his art studio, calling it 'The Factory'. The name itself reflected how differently he approached art production and changed the whole concept of what being an artist meant. Rather than being a space for him to work alone, it became a venue which attracted other creative minds to come and work collaboratively with him under his direction. It was an environment in which Warhol felt at ease, because he was in his element, and for the artists that joined him, it was a fantastic place to explore new concepts, discuss radical ideas and to just think.

Huge volumes of work came out of the Factory. As well as mass producing his famous silk screen prints, Warhol branched out into a wide variety of other media, including painting, drawing, sculpture and film. In each of the different media that he worked, and indeed for each individual piece, he strived to create something new and original.

As his fame grew, he built on his success by cultivating a powerful public image of himself with his trademark white wig and dark glasses, which became the Andy Warhol 'brand'. He single-handedly created his own celebrity profile and was photo-documenting his life too – decades before Instagram – using a polaroid camera. The dedication to this 'photo diary' saw Warhol go through a whole roll of film every day for an entire decade.

His desire for creativity and originality often resulted in bizarre projects. For instance, his film *The Empire State Building* lasted eight hours and was simply a film of the building with its lights going on and off. According to Warhol, the purpose of the art piece was "to see time go by". Another, called *Sleep*, was simply a film of the poet John Gioron sleeping for six hours.

Warhol's boundless creative energy never waned and he continued to experiment with as many different media as possible, ranging from prints and video diaries to soap operas and music videos. He even turned to rock music, managing and producing the experimental rock band the Velvet Underground. However, his legacy will surely be his iconic images of soup cans and celebrities.

In February 1987, at the age of 58, Warhol passed away following surgery for persistent gallbladder problems.

Autistic traits

Visual thinking
A man of few words, Warhol expressed his views, feelings and questions about life through the medium of striking visual imagery. According to Temple Grandin visual thinking is one of three classic autistic cognitive types, along with pattern thinkers (maths and music) and verbal specialists (writers and poets).

Special interests
His early obsession with movie stars and Hollywood culture, together with his love of different art forms, led to a lifelong passion for producing art that reflected American culture. He was a workaholic, often working day and night pursuing art in one form or another, but this was his life and what he loved to do. Every aspect of his life and anything that caught his eye, he would turn into art. Continually experimenting with different mediums, he painted, printed, photographed, filmed and recorded everything around him so that his whole life became synonymous with his work. They were one and the same.

Out of the box thinking

A theme that ran throughout his career was Warhol's constant search for new ways of exploring the very concept of art. One of Warhol's radical ideas was that the stuff of modern life could be art, whether it be Campbell's soup cans or washing powder boxes.

He continually challenged the very definition of art, was never restricted by traditional artistic methods and techniques, and was always exploring the use of new mediums for artistic projects. Whichever medium he worked with, Warhol would strive to be unconventional, blurring the lines between art and creativity such that creativity became art in its own right. The act of creating novel imagery was, for him, pure art. For example, the movies he produced were shown without editing; they would run from anything between three minutes and 24 hours and would be shown exactly as they came out of the camera, complete with scratches and specks of dust.

Warhol's art was also used as a way to chronicle some of the time's most important events, including the assassination of John F Kennedy, the death of Marilyn Monroe and Mao Tse Tung's rule in China.

Lack of understanding of status and social etiquette

Securing his first assignment in New York by simply walking into the offices of Glamour magazine and asking to see the editor is not how young, inexperienced illustrators would normally try to get a job. Yet showing his portfolio to a potential employer and letting his art do the talking, rather than him having to talk about his work, turned out to be the perfect way for Warhol to get attention.

Poor social skills

As a child, Warhol found it difficult to form friendships and didn't have any close friends. In his autobiography he writes "I wasn't very close to anyone, although I guess I wanted to be ... I felt left out".[1]

Even as an adult, he refused to indulge in small talk and was very economical with his words. When he did talk, it was nearly always about his work. However, because of his artistic accomplishments, creativity and talents, he was surrounded by collaborators and admirers, which meant that despite his poor social skills he had an active social life. Attending parties was part and parcel of his role as a popular artist, but even in these purely social environments he remained quiet and shy, choosing instead to attend as an observer. This is a splendid example of how expertise in a subject, whether it be art, music, or sport, can open doors into the social world and help alleviate some of the social difficulties that autistic people experience.

Communication difficulties

Warhol's problems with speech started from an early age and resulted in him being frequently tongue-tied. Recalling his struggles, he said "...and sometimes in the middle of a sentence I feel like a foreigner trying to talk it (sic) because I have word spasms where the parts of some words begin to sound peculiar to me".[2] However, he more than overcame his language difficulties with his amazing ability to communicate visually. In his case, a picture really was worth a thousand words.

Awkward appearance

Warhol usually appeared uncomfortable, distant and aloof in interviews and even photographs didn't project the confident image of an artist at the top of his profession. This apparent indifference is a very common autistic trait; yet behind this seemingly blank expression, Warhol was actually incredibly analytical, intellectual and perceptive, with a warm, kind-hearted nature. He liked to help people who were less fortunate than him and was well known for volunteering at homeless shelters across New York.

Sensory cravings

Warhol enjoyed going to the dry cleaners and would often stand in the corner just to relish the smell of the chemicals and sounds of the cleaning machines. Another curious craving he had was to go through airport security multiple times – he found it fascinating.

A love of routine and repetition

Despite his work revolving around novelty and change, he personally liked the reliability of sameness, supposedly lunching on Campbell's soup and crackers every single day for 20 years. He would play the same pop records over, and over, and over again, and in his autobiography confirmed his desire for predictability by stating "All the Cokes are the same and all the Cokes are good".[3]

An obsessional collector of things

He was a lifelong hoarder and after his death, in 1988, it took nine days to auction off his immense collection of random objects, including 175 cookie jars, 610 time capsules (cardboard boxes containing a random collection of his everyday items) and an abundance of Miss Piggy memorabilia. The sale raised $25 million and formed the basis of the Andy Warhol Foundation for the Visual Arts, which supports up-and-coming artists.

What has Andy Warhol done for us?

Warhol redefined the very concept of what art is by showing us that art doesn't have to be constrained by a box based on traditional ideas of art. He opened our minds to new possibilities and challenged us to think differently. When people look at Constable's *The Hay Wain* for example, they admire his skill and the beauty of the painting. When confronted with a painting of a soup can, it takes the mind into completely new territory.

By using his outstanding artistic talents and very skilled eye, Warhol transformed everyday objects and seemingly ordinary pictures of famous people into works of art as a parody of America's obsessions with mass consumerism, glamour and celebrities. Did he do this because he was exploring the possibilities of what art itself could be, or to bring to our attention the shallowness of American values, or was he simply reflecting on the people and events that mattered at the time? We will never know and that is the beauty of great art – it provokes great debate about what the art is actually saying and is open to interpretation by the observer.

His influence is still seen everywhere; from the work of modern day artists to reality TV, and even in photo and video sharing apps, like Instagram. Warhol's philosophy was summed up neatly by Jeremy Deller, an artist who worked with Warhol: "As an artist, you can make your own world, you can do exactly what you want and anything you're interested in can become art".[4]

Star Trek's Mr Spock

Spock is the second fictional character I've included in this book, and again, the reason for mentioning him is that he is a person we all know about who displays some prominent autistic traits.

We recognise that Spock is different from us, and yet we like him, we admire him and we absolutely acknowledge that he is a vitally important crew member of the Star Trek Enterprise. The underlying message of *Star Trek* is that diversity can not only work effectively, but that a team player who thinks differently can be invaluable. In other words, Spock is a perfect example of how neurodiversity can provide huge benefits.

We can see straight away that Spock is different from us, because his pointy ears tell us he's half Vulcan and so we anticipate that his behaviour will probably be different too. Being *visibly* different (as well as half alien!) acts as a catalyst by helping anyone that meets him immediately realise that he isn't like everyone else. With autism there are no physical differences, which is why it's often referred to as a 'hidden', or 'invisible' condition and this understandably makes it considerably harder for people to accommodate us.

Spock is an all-too-rare positive role model for autistic people, promoting, as he does, the value of autistic attributes and reframing negative stereotypes of autism in a more positive light.

Why is he famous?

Spock is the Science Officer on board the Starship Enterprise in the science fiction *Star Trek* series of TV shows and films. The Starship's mission is "to explore strange new worlds, to seek out new life and new civilizations, to boldly go where no man has gone before". The first showing was in 1966 and, due to its immense popularity, there have been seven spin-off television series, two animated series, 13 films, video games and new adaptations continuing to be made today. *Star Trek* has developed a huge fan base and Spock, apart from being an alien, is particularly famous for his outstanding logical brain.

How did Star Trek come about?

Star Trek was the first TV programme to bring together a wide range of diverse characters and show how they could all work together as a team to accomplish great things exploring new civilisations in outer space. This was a dramatic departure from the conservative TV of the time – the crew included not only an alien, but also a Japanese and a Russian character, both of whom were sworn enemies of the USA at the time, and it was the first time a black woman had a major role in a popular TV show. The show painted a utopian future in which a variety of races and species all live and work together in harmony, which I find truly inspiring.

Gene Roddenberry, the creator of *Star Trek*, said he wanted *Star Trek* to "show what humanity might develop into, if it would learn from the lessons of the past".[1] He set out to produce a show where multi-cultural diversity existed in complete harmony, yet the producers initially expressed concerns about marketability and opposed Roddenberry's insistence that the show should have a racially diverse cast. Fortunately, Roddenberry's views triumphed. To make the show even more interesting and relevant, many of the conflicts and political dimensions of *Star Trek* were allegories of contemporary cultural events.

Spock's character

Spock was the son of a human mother and a Vulcan father. Standing at six feet tall with pointed ears, slanted eyebrows, a distinct hairstyle cut boldly across the forehead and a slightly greenish-tinged complexion due to the copper content in his blood, his appearance was striking to say the least. He was typically very thoughtful, reserved and took great pride in his logical thinking.

Spock inherited his very logical approach from his father, yet at times would have some internal conflict with his emotional side due to his human mother. For him, showing emotion would be highly embarrassing, as it was considered unacceptable in Vulcan culture to do so.

Spock was exceptionally intelligent and extremely knowledgeable about human history and human nature. He was dependable, obsessive about getting things right and a trustworthy member of the crew that everyone knew they could rely on.

Autistic Traits

Extremely logical way of thinking

Spock always adopts a purely logical approach to every situation. He looks at all the available facts and analyses the data before deciding on the optimum course of action.

In *The Gamesters of Trikelion* episode, for example, Spock has to take command when the Captain and two crew members have beamed off the ship and appear to be lost. Spock discovers a faint ion trail, and orders the ship to follow it despite the protests of Chief Medical Officer Dr McCoy, who says in an exasperated way:

> "You're going to leave here without them and run off on some wild goose chase halfway across the galaxy just because you've found a discrepancy in a hydrogen cloud?"

> "Doctor, I am chasing the Captain, Lieutenant Uhuru and ensign Chekov – not some wild aquatic fowl. This is the only lead we have" is Spock's calm reply.

Spock even quotes one of Sherlock Holmes' most famous lines in *Star Trek VI: The Undiscovered Country*, describing his logical way of thinking by saying "An ancestor of mine maintained that if you eliminate the impossible, whatever remains, however improbable, must be the solution".

Literal thinker

Spock takes comments as they are said without reading more into them. For example in *The Immunity Syndrome* episode, when Captain Kirk thinks Spock has died and then hears his voice, he exclaims:

> "Spock – you're alive!" to which Spock replies:

"Obviously Captain."

In another episode Kirk asks Mr Chekov:

> "How close will we come to the nearest Klingon outpost if we continue on this course?"

> "1 parsec – close enough to smell them" replies Chekov, to which Spock comments:

> "That is illogical – odours cannot travel through the vacuum of space."

Socially unaware

He is often blunt and direct, does not see the point of any social niceties and cuts right to the heart of the matter in question. He doesn't intentionally offend anyone and fortunately he is amongst people who understand that this is his nature, so he is able to flourish and excel at his job in this accepting environment.

Emotionally detached

The director of *Star Trek*, Joseph Sargent, specifically wanted Spock to "Be different. Be the scientist. Be detached", to see a situation as "something that's a curiosity rather than a threat".[2] In a scene when the ship was threatened by an outside force, the Captain was issuing commands and people were reacting by scurrying around, Spock simply assessed the situation and said one word: "Fascinating".[2] This response was one of Spock's standard responses to any dangerous situation where the rest of the crew are fearing for their lives. Spock remains calm and emotionally detached and simply assesses the available data.

Attention to detail

In combination with his logic, Spock's attention to detail ensures he makes astute appraisals of situations. He is very observant, noticing patterns and changes which others may miss. He is very accurate and precise in his observations to the point of being pedantic. For example in *The Omega Glory*, Captain Kirk has been knocked unconscious. When he comes round he asks Spock how long he was out for: "seven hours and eight minutes Captain" is Spock's reply.

Total honesty

He gains the trust of all the crew members because they know exactly where they stand with him due to the fact that he is totally honest at all times. However, sometimes his comments may not be complementary and he comes across as being 'brutally honest'. For example, in *Day of the Dove* he says "May I say that I have not thoroughly enjoyed serving with humans? I find their illogic and foolish emotions a constant irritant".

Total loyalty

He is a committed crew member of the StarShip Enterprise and is totally dedicated to serving the fleet, the ship and the Captain. Even though he often misunderstands human motivations, he is considered genuine and loyal and is immensely valued by those around him. He states in the film *Star Trek: Into Darkness*: "It is my function aboard this ship to advise you in making the wisest decisions possible".

Special interest

Spock's special interest is science and therefore he is ideally suited to his role as science officer on board the ship. He displays great curiosity, fascination and wonder for discovery of any kind.

What has Mr Spock done for us?

Spock has shown us a world in which difference is not only totally accepted, but highly valued. In the various *Star Trek* series and films, the central theme always revolves around a crew of very diverse people working together; each crew member brings a specific set of skills and expertise to the table which, when combined, makes for an unbeatable team.

Mankind today is facing various issues that threaten our very existence – climate change, pollution, biodiversity loss and pandemics. We need all the help we can get and it seems to me that in light of the insights about the autistic way of thinking outlined in this book, it would be foolish to ignore the contribution autistic people can make towards this effort. As Spock once said:

> Nowhere am I more desperately needed than on a shipload of illogical humans.[3]

Temple Grandin (1947 –)

One of the simplest ways to describe autism is that it's a different way of processing information. Temple Grandin is a visual thinker who processes the world in images rather than words. She also describes herself as a bottom-up thinker – most people look at the bigger picture first and then pay attention to the details; however she studies the details first and then compiles her own big picture. According to Grandin, this leads to a unique benefit: more innovative thoughts and ideas, unconstrained by preconceived ideas, or having to fit in with social rules.

As we shall see, Grandin is a perfect example of finding your place in the world, your raison d'être. Like her, I've found a career that suits me and my autistic skills. Also, like her, I'm able to communicate what it's like being autistic to neurotypicals – I see myself as sitting on the fence between the autistic and the neurotypical worlds. We both try to inspire other autistic people, parents, professionals and employers with our talks, books, articles and webinars. We both emphasise what autistic people *can* do rather than what they *can't* do (unlike almost every other article I read about autism.)

Grandin is a person to be admired *because* she had substantial difficulties as a child (due to her autism), yet she overcame them and became a world leading expert in her chosen field of study. She then found that she could tell people about her experiences and inspire them to follow their interests and capitalise on their strengths.

Why is she famous?

Temple Grandin is a best-selling author, professor of animal sciences and an inspiration to millions of people around the world. She is well known for her trailblazing work as a spokesperson for autistic people and was one of the first autistic individuals to write a first-hand account of her life and experiences, at a time when many thought autistic people were incapable of self-understanding, or describing how they felt and experienced the world. Her life's work has been to understand her own autistic mind and this has aided her in her work with animal behaviour; she is one of the most respected experts in both autism and animal behaviour in the world.

She tours extensively giving talks on autism, inspiring autistic people by showing them what can be achieved, despite the difficulties they encounter. In recognition of her achievements, Grandin was named in the 'Heroes' category of Time Magazine's 100 most influential people in the world in 2010.

Childhood

Grandin displayed many classic autistic traits as a child. She was a late speaker, wouldn't make eye contact, had a fixation for spinning objects, preferred to be alone, experienced many sensory issues and disliked being held. Being unable to communicate what she was feeling resulted in a violent temper with bouts of continuous screaming.

Her mother was advised to send Grandin to an institution, but was so convinced her daughter had potential she sent her to a regular high school. Here, Grandin described herself as the "nerdy kid" whom everyone ridiculed.[1] The kids would tease her relentlessly until she hit out at them and was then expelled. Her next school was a special boarding school for gifted children with emotional problems. It had a stable and horses for the pupils to ride, which marked a turning point in her life; she felt at one with animals and would spend every minute she could possibly spare with the horses.

As well as her passion for animals, she developed a profound interest in science. She found the technical language as easy as the social language was difficult. Thanks to a few dedicated teachers and her mother's faith in her, she excelled in the sciences at school. Prior to her science teacher's recognition of her talents and his encouragement, she had been considered a poor student, bored and unmotivated.

Another supportive figure was her Aunt Ann, who could see Grandin had potential but was struggling to fit in. Grandin would spend the summer holidays at her ranch in Arizona and it was here that she realised that she could relate to animals far easier than she could to humans. She felt completely at ease when riding horses, or tending to cattle, and even found that she could communicate with them, reading their moods and talking to them. She would spend hours like this, just watching the cattle and observing their behaviour. At vaccination time they would be herded into the cattle chute leading to a cattle restraining device, which kept them still to receive their injection. She saw how alarmed they were, because they had no idea what was about to happen, but as soon as the restraining panels were gently pressed against their sides, they would calm down.

It dawned on her that this was exactly what *she* needed to overcome her own levels of anxiety. She was so convinced about this that she set about building one for herself. This 'squeeze machine', as she named it, allowed her to control the level of physical pressure she needed in order to feel calmer; like a hug without having to tolerate another person's touch. The effect was both stimulating and relaxing at the same time and she still uses one to this day. She says that being able to reduce her levels of stress and anxiety absolutely transformed her life.

Adult Life

Grandin's love of animals and her first hand experiences on her aunt's ranch developed into a special interest in cattle-handling facilities. This was a difficult field to go into, particularly for a female, but she was a determined and tenacious young woman – once she was fixated on a goal, she would do all that was required in order to achieve it.

Instead of designing a cattle handling facility from the starting point of efficiency and cost effectiveness, she looked at it from the animal's point of view and found ways to make the experience as easy and incident free as possible. This resulted in more humane treatment and less stress for the animals, which ultimately led to less disruption, making for a smoother and more cost effective operation.

These improved facilities were so much better than previous versions that today over half the cattle in the United States and Canada are handled in the chute systems that Grandin designed. She has been honoured as a 'visionary' by the organisation People for the Ethical Treatment of Animals (PETA) for making cattle-processing plants more humane.

A career in animal handling turned out to be ideally suited to her as this combined her deep understanding of animal behaviour with her outstanding visual thinking. To date, she has published over 300 scientific papers and her website gets 5,000 visitors each month. She currently works as a Professor of Animal Science at Colorado State

University and tours the world presenting lectures on animal management.

Outside the field of animal science, Grandin is known worldwide for her ability to communicate what it's actually like to be autistic, which has made her the person who has probably had *the* biggest impact on the world's understanding of autism. Her first autism conference was in the mid 1980s at the National Society for Autistic Children in Chicago. For the first time, the audience heard an autistic adult relate her experiences of being extremely sensitive to certain sounds, how as a child she couldn't verbally articulate how painful a clothes label could be due to her profound skin sensitivity and the difficulties she had in understanding relationships with people. To hear a first-hand account of life with autism was a revelation. And in 1986, following this success, she wrote *Emergence: Labeled Autistic*, the first book written by an autistic individual about living with the condition.

She's since published many other books about autism having dedicated enormous time and effort to understanding her condition and then translating her experiences for others to learn from. Reading and hearing about the condition first hand from someone highly articulate and practical has given parents and professionals a much better idea of how to bring up and support autistic children. This in turn leads to much better outcomes. She is now an acclaimed autistic speaker with her talks having been viewed millions of times online.

In 2010 her life was made into an Emmy Award-winning movie, *Temple Grandin*. On top of that, she's also featured in many major television programmes, from the BBC special, *The Woman Who Thinks Like a Cow*, to ABC's *Primetime Live*, *The Today Show*, *Larry King Live*, *48 Hours*, and *20/20*. To this day, she continues to be active in the field of autism, always encouraging autistic people to utilise their strengths by pursuing their special interests.

Autistic traits

Extraordinary powers of visual thinking

Grandin is an exceptional visual thinker, which is one of the reasons for the success of her novel and efficient livestock handling installations. She runs 'simulations' in her head to test run the equipment and imagine exactly what it will be like for the cattle when they enter a chute. She describes the process as being rather like a virtual reality computer program running in her head. This allows her to preview any potential problems and make any necessary adaptations at the design stage. She didn't actually realise that this was a special skill until much later in her career and was quite amazed to discover that non-autistic equipment designers didn't run full motion test simulations of equipment in their minds.

Exceptional attention to detail

Being a primarily visual thinker means she sees details that others miss – she considers this an essential requirement for designing humane animal handling equipment. In her book, *Animals in Translation: Using the Mysteries of Autism to Decode Animal Behaviour,* she says that it's the small details that make all the difference between an animal facility working well, or being inoperable. Animals notice visual details and Grandin would 'see' the facility through their eyes, allowing her to take into account every minute detail that affected them, which most other people simply wouldn't notice. She would get down on her hands and knees to be at the same level as a pig for example, and then see lots of tiny, bright reflections glancing off the wet floor, which was disturbing for pigs and would stop them from proceeding along a chute. There could be shadows and shafts of light shining through bars, slippery flooring, jiggling chains, metal clanging, high-pitched sounds like hissing air, a piece of clothing hanging up nearby – lots of seemingly minor details to us, but they are factors that could be major issues to the animal.

Persistence

Grandin is extremely hard working and has immense determination and willingness to stick at things, despite sometimes receiving criticism and rejection. This tenacity is one of the key reasons why she has become a world expert in the field of livestock handling.

Special interest

Her work is her life – the two are inextricably bound. She has written that almost all of her social contacts are with livestock people, or people interested in autism and most of her evenings are spent either writing papers, or sketching new ideas for animal handling facilities. Even her 'extracurricular' interests are factual, with any recreational reading consisting mostly of science and livestock publications.

Matter of fact manner

One reason her first book is so informative is that it's written with total openness and honesty with absolutely no concern about what people may think about her. It is a starkly factual account of her life and her thought processes at the time. She is direct and forthright and is totally accepting of the fact that she is different to most people.

However, she is willing to learn social courtesies in order to get on in the world. For example, she relates how she was once working on a new facility and told one of the workers that his weld was "like a pigeon had doo-dah'd on it".[2] The foreman asked her to come into the office and suggested she should be more tactful in future.

She has a loud, unmodulated voice and on being interviewed in a diner by Bernard Rimland, he felt compelled to ask her to lower her voice, to which she wasn't the slightest bit offended. She fully recognises her oddities – the peculiarities of her speech and manners – but rather than be self-conscious, or embarrassed, she regards them as obstacles to be overcome.

Sensory issues
She dislikes being hugged by people, but likes the feeling of controlled pressure, hence the squeeze machine she built as a self-calming mechanism. She is also sound sensitive and finds background noises disturbing; a fan whirring, or the sound of a vacuum cleaner being almost unbearable. However, she uses her different way of processing sensory information to her advantage when trying to understand how animals see, think and feel and takes this into account when designing and improving animal facilities.

Late speaker
A delay in the development of speech is very common in autistic children and this is something that Grandin displayed – she didn't begin to talk until she was nearly four years old.

Echolalia
Repeating phrases is another common autistic trait and at school her peers called her "Tape recorder", as she would store up a lot of phrases in her head and then say them over and over again in every conversation.[3]

Uneven profile
A defining feature of autism is to display an uneven profile. In common with most of the characters in this book, Grandin had a very mixed school record. She was terrible at the subjects that she was bored with and saw no point in learning, but an exceptional student when the topic interested her.

Poor social skills
At school, she struggled to fit in because of her lack of social skills. To this day, she finds socialising difficult and sees little point in social niceties, or small talk, always getting straight to the matter in hand. But, over the years she has persevered with this particular obstacle,

learning how to respond or behave in certain situations simply through experience, so her social skills have improved considerably.

She's always found forming human relationships difficult, so lives alone. This works well for her, as she's made a conscious decision to devote her whole life to animal welfare and raising awareness of autism.

Difficulty empathising

She finds it hard to understand other people's emotions and, being a *Star Trek* fan, she has said that she identifies with both Spock and Data. In an interview she described the episode when the crew of the Star Trek Enterprise were prepared to endanger themselves to recover the body of a dead crew member. Spock did not consider this to be logical and neither did Grandin: "But I learnt that emotions will often overpower logical thinking, even if these decisions prove hazardous".[4]

Logical thinker

Logic dictates Grandin's life simply because she has no understanding of any other viewpoint: "I see how people fight over stupid things. Not thinking logically. I'm kind of appalled at just how irrational humans can be".[5]

What has Temple Grandin done for us?

Grandin has shown the world that when autistic people play to their strengths, they can become world experts in their chosen field. She is a shining example of how the autistic trait of pursuing obsessive interests with focus and determination can lead to significant achievements. Most importantly, she was one of the first people to eloquently communicate to the world what it's like to be autistic which has helped promote greater understanding of autism and led to more acceptance and tolerance of neurodiversity.

She's an inspiring ambassador for the autistic community and her positive message has made a tremendous difference to the lives of thousands of autistic people. And, she's also made a huge improvement to the lives of millions of animals by revolutionising the way cattle are handled.

Steve Jobs (1955 – 2011)

Steve Jobs embraced the idea that people who thought differently could bring huge benefits to his company. And, as Apple is currently one of the most valuable businesses in the world, it looks as if he was right. Most employers hire people who think like them because they feel comfortable surrounded by those who have similar viewpoints and ways of thinking. However, Jobs was fully aware that divergent thinking could produce more sophisticated and novel solutions which would give the company a competitive edge.

A perfect example of this is the Apple advert he commissioned in 1997:

> Here's to the crazy ones, the misfits, the rebels, the troublemakers, the round pegs in the square holes... the ones who see things differently – they're not fond of rules... You can quote them, disagree with them, glorify or vilify them, but the only thing you can't do is ignore them because they change things... they push the human race forward, and while some may see them as the crazy ones, we see genius, because the ones who are crazy enough to

think that they can change the world are the ones who do.[1]

Why is he famous?

Steve Jobs is a global icon who shaped the worlds of technology and media. He co-founded Apple Computers, the American technology company that introduced the first personal computer (PC) in colour to the home market – a revolution in computing at the time. The iPod followed next, a versatile portable music player, and then the iPhone, which changed how people communicate and access information all over the world. He also started a company named Pixar which went on to produce the world's first computer animated feature film, *Toy Story*. In other words, computers, music accessibility, mobile phones and movies have all been totally transformed by Steve Jobs.

Childhood

Steve Jobs was adopted as a baby by Paul and Clara Jobs. They were extremely supportive and loving parents; so much so that Jobs never liked them being referred to as adoptive parents, as he considered them to be his parents "1000%".[2]

He was a curious child, but school bored him and he didn't function well in the traditional education system. But, he loved reading and one teacher, Mrs Hill, noticed his natural intellect and understood his unwillingness to conform. With a unique approach, tailored just for Jobs, she was able to inspire and challenge him – she even bought him various learning kits for projects like building his own camera. Steve later acknowledged her efforts by saying "I learned more that year than I think I learned in any year in school".[3] This is a great example of how the right support for kids who don't fit in can transform their lives.

Steve became one of the best students in his class and, as a result, he was able to skip a grade. Unfortunately, this meant he was the youngest in his new class making it difficult for him to make friends. He was perceived as a loner, which soon started the bullying by his peers. Eventually he couldn't take it anymore and point blank refused to go back to school.

Keen to do what was best for him, his parents agreed to move out of the area, so that Steve could have a fresh start. They bought a house in Los Altos, a city in Santa Clara County, California. This area had long been a major site of research and technology for the US navy (in 1909 it was home to the first radio station in the United States). After World War II, Stanford University set up a scheme to encourage graduates to start their own companies and in 1951 the Stanford Industrial Park was created whereby the University leased portions of its land to high-tech firms. This nurtured companies like Hewlett-Packard, Eastman Kodak, General Electric, Lockheed Corporation and other high-tech firms. Eventually, what would later become known as Silicon Valley grew up around the Stanford University campus. Vacuum tube manufacturing was also pioneered here, and it was *the* hub for 'ham' (amateur) radio enthusiasts who had been trained in the local technology companies.

This was an ideal environment for the young Steve to grow up in; a neighbourhood full of hobbyists, technology geeks and entrepreneurs, just the kind of people he got on with.

At the age of 12, he read an article in *Scientific American*, which sparked a key idea in him that ultimately led to the computer revolution that changed the world. The study measured the efficiency of locomotion for a number of species on planet earth i.e. how much energy they expended to get from point A to point B. The winner was the condor, a type of vulture and the largest American bird. However, humans were only about a third of the way down the list. The study then tested the efficiency of a human riding a bicycle, which blew away the condor. This made a really big impression on Steve. It demonstrated that humans are tool builders – we can fashion tools that amplify our inherent abilities to spectacular magnitudes. It occurred to him that a computer could be considered to be a "bicycle of the mind", a tool to take us far beyond our inherent abilities. [4]

One day, he visited a NASA centre near to his home, where he saw his first computer – in this case, a remote terminal connected to a main computer somewhere else. Steve was utterly fascinated by it and this motivated him to join the Electronics club at his school, Homestead High. The club arranged visits to the local Hewlett Packard Explorers Club, which met in the HP cafeteria and featured HP engineers talking about their projects. As an adult, the trip held great memories for him:

> I saw my first desktop computer there. It was called the 9100A, and it was a glorified calculator, but also really the first desktop computer. It was huge, maybe 40 pounds, but it was a beauty of a thing. I fell in love with it. [5]

Steve was becoming known for his determination to do things for himself and his rebellious, nonconforming nature was also no doubt influenced by the 60s counterculture – he loved the Beatles and Bob Dylan and grew his hair long. Terry Anzur, a girl he was at school with, recalls that Homestead High "wasn't much different from any American high school where teens are categorized and stereotyped on the way to the rest of their lives. Steve followed his own path, and that made him kind of an outsider with those who followed the crowd. He did, however, make an impression in the senior talent contest by putting on a laser light show at a time when most of us had never even heard of lasers". [6]

Steve became friends with another boy who lived near him – Steve Wozniak, or "Woz", as he was known to his friends. Steve greatly admired Woz, largely because he was the first person that he had met who knew more about electronics than he did. Despite the fact that Woz went to college at Berkeley and Steve attended Homestead High School, they were kindred spirits and met frequently.

They also worked together on a prank project which involved making and selling 'blue boxes': homemade machines that allowed users to make long-distance phone calls anywhere in the world without paying any money. Woz once prank-called the Pope at the Vatican and pretended to be Secretary of State, Henry Kissinger. These were two minds that, when put together, were unstoppable and Jobs wasn't ignorant of the fact:

> We were so fascinated by them (blue boxes) that Woz and I figured out how to build one. We built the best one in the world; the first digital blue box in the world. We would give them to our friends and use them ourselves. And you know, you rapidly run out of people you want to call. But it was the magic that two teenagers could build this box for $100 worth of parts and control hundreds of billions of dollars of infrastructure in the entire telephone network in the whole world. Experiences like that taught us the power of ideas. If it hadn't been for the blue boxes, there would be no Apple. I'm 100 percent sure of that. [7]

In 1972, he attended Reed College in Portland, Oregon. But, just six months into his degree, he made the decision to drop out because he didn't feel the course was value for money, especially as the high tuition fees were using all of his working-class parents' savings. Luckily for him, the college allowed students to attend courses of their choice on an ad hoc basis for greatly reduced fees. This meant that he could stop taking the classes that didn't interest him and only attend the ones that did. One said class was calligraphy, which greatly impacted Apple's design work Jobs later recalled:

167

I decided to take a calligraphy class. I learned about serif and sans-serif typefaces, about varying the space between different letter combinations, about what makes great typography great. It was beautiful. Historical. Artistically subtle in a way that science can't capture. And I found it fascinating. None of this had any hope of any practical application in my life. But 10 years later, when we were designing the first Macintosh computer, it all came back to me. And we designed it all into the Mac. It was the first computer with beautiful typography. If I had never dropped in on that single course in college, the Mac would never have multiple typefaces or proportionally spaced fonts. And since Windows just copied the Mac, it's likely that no personal computer would have them.[8]

Adult Life

On leaving college, Jobs returned home and joined Atari Corporation as a video game designer. He met up with Steve Wozniak again and started attending the Homebrew Computer Club – a "ragtag group of geeky misfits".[9] Wozniak, a technical genius, had designed a prototype user-friendly 'personal' computer and Jobs immediately saw the potential of the machine. They decided to try and persuade the companies they worked for (Wozniak was at Hewlett Packard) to hire the other one and let them work together developing this innovative product. Both employers turned them down – if only they knew what was to come! Giving up was not an option for Jobs, so he and Wozniak decided to go it alone, starting their own company.

In early 1976, they produced the first Apple 1 computer in Jobs' parent's garage using money obtained by selling their most valuable possessions – Jobs' Volkswagen minibus (Jobs figured he could ride around on his bicycle if he had to) and Wozniak's programmable calculator. With a characteristic sense of humour, they founded Apple Computer on April Fool's Day, 1 April 1976. Jobs said later that they gave Apple the name partly because he liked apples, and "partially because Apple is ahead of Atari in the phone book and I used to work at Atari".[10]

They worked tirelessly together over the next year and then released the Apple II, which revolutionised the computer industry with the introduction of colour graphics. It was one of the first highly successful mass-produced personal computers and Apple soon became the fastest growing company of all time. Sales increased from $7.8 million in 1978 to a whopping $117 million in 1980. It was also the first company to sell over a million computers.

Wozniak left Apple in 1983 due to his lack of interest in the everyday running of the company. In his place, Jobs hired PepsiCo's John Scully as president, using his phenomenal powers of persuasion to bring him on board. In true Jobs style, he simply said "Do you want to sell sugared water for the rest of your life? Or do you want to come with me and change the world?".[11] However, they had major disagreements about which products Apple should concentrate on and Jobs was forced to leave in 1985. The blow devastated Jobs – he had built up the company from scratch, with his whole life now revolving around Apple and its products.

But determination and dogged persistence are typical characteristics of most entrepreneurs and Jobs was no exception. He still loved what he did and so, undaunted, he began working on how to turn disaster into opportunity. It transpired that leaving Apple freed him to enter one of the most creative periods of his life. He started a new company, NeXT Software, and also took over the struggling computer animation company, Pixar, which went on to produce the first computer animated feature film, *Toy Story*. A household name, Pixar is now the most successful animation studio in the world.

In a remarkable turn of events, Apple then bought NeXT in 1997 (they wanted its operating system) and Jobs found himself back at the company he had founded. Apple was struggling at this stage and its future was uncertain. Jobs secured a $150 million injection from Microsoft, restructured the company and reduced its bloated product line by 70%, thus regaining profitability and starting a spectacular revival of Apple's fortunes. His comeback is widely believed to have brought about the biggest corporate turnaround in the history of America.

Jobs' visionary ideas projected the company to new heights. Apple branched out into music related products with the iPod music players and then the iTunes music store. This was a tremendous advance on both the popular Sony Walkman portable cassette player and the ubiquitous CDs, both of which could only hold a dozen or so songs.

The original iPod was able to hold 1,000 songs, was 0.2 inches thick and came with Apple's own FireWire cable that let users import songs onto their iPods. "This is a quantum leap because for most people [1,000 songs] is their entire music library," explained Jobs. "You can take your whole music library with you right in your pocket".[12]

Perhaps the smartest thing Apple did with the iPod was to tightly integrate it into the iTunes interface and iTunes Store, making Apple the go-to source for buying and managing music on the web. This morphed into Apple's core business strategy: making 'entertainment hubs' on which consumers could store and access their music, movies, books and other media. It didn't just change the way we all listen to music; it changed the entire music industry.

Then in 2007 Jobs presented possibly the most remarkable product launch in the history of technology, giving it the following introduction:

Every once in a while a revolutionary product comes along that changes everything. Well, today, we're introducing three revolutionary products of this class:

The first one: is a widescreen iPod with touch controls.
The second: is a revolutionary mobile phone.
And the third is a breakthrough Internet communications device.
An iPod, a phone, and an Internet communicator. An iPod, a phone ... Are you getting it?
These are not three separate devices, this is *one* device, and we are calling it the iPhone.[13]

He then proceeded to demonstrate it. The 'scrolling' feature drew audible gasps from the audience and the 'pinch-to-zoom' capability was applauded with incredulity. We take these things for granted now, but at the time no one had ever seen anything like it. On top of all this, it looked like something straight out of a science fiction film. A tablet, with no buttons, was as mysterious as alien technology would have been. Competitors' smartphones, such as the original Blackberry – akin to clunky pocket calculators combining a full keyboard of physical buttons with a tiny screen – suddenly looked like museum pieces.

It was hugely successful with immediate effect. Not only because of its amazing functionality, but also because its beautiful design made it desirable – people didn't just *need* one they *wanted* one. The last public sales figures Apple issued in November 2018 stated that 2.2 billion iPhones had been sold worldwide (Apple has since stopped providing sales data).

Jobs was diagnosed with pancreatic cancer in 2003 but continued to work until his death at the age of 56 in 2011. His most pertinent quote, for me, was "The ones who see things differently...they change things... they push the human race forward".[1] And that he did.

Autistic traits

Out of the box thinking
Steve Jobs had the autistic tendency to 'think outside of the box' in abundance. This incredible capability enabled him to create products that changed the world, for example:

- The Macintosh – the first affordable personal computer that used the now ubiquitous window-and-mouse system. "It was obvious to me that every computer in the world would work this way someday"[14] Jobs later said.
- The iPhone – incorporating over 200 separate new patents, the iPhone wasn't just one revolutionary idea, it was over 200!

Intense passion
Jobs was obsessive about his interests and was known in his youth both for his love of gadgets and his fanatical enthusiasm for music. This passion continued throughout his career. An Apple employee described him as being "like the most excited kid in the world about Apple and their cool stuff".[15]

He was so committed and involved in his work at Apple that he actually loved the products he helped design. His overriding enthusiasm was apparent in the new product releases that Jobs personally presented. When he first announced the new iPhone 4 to the world, he said "Believe me – you've gotta see this thing in person. It is one of the most beautiful designs you've ever seen!".[16] This wasn't just sales talk, he really meant it.

His work was like an all-consuming hobby. Even though he put in ridiculous hours and earned lots of money, it wasn't actually work for him:

> I was worth a million dollars when I was twenty-three and over ten million dollars when I was twenty-four, and over a hundred million dollars when I was twenty-five. It wasn't that important because I never did it for the money.[17]

Poor social skills

He was, without doubt, confrontational. Jobs would say it as it is very clearly and directly, with no concern for other people's feelings. If he had a goal in mind, he would do everything needed to achieve that goal, irrelevant of upsetting people along the way.

There aren't many Apple employees that would describe him as easy to work with. For example, he would be extremely blunt and critical of people's work in meetings. However afterwards they would almost always say that he was right and agree that 'good enough' was not acceptable – they had to come up with something great. Despite this total lack of social niceties, the people he employed at Apple tolerated his eccentric behaviour and were extremely dedicated and loyal. Not one employee left the company in its first few years of operation, which is quite a remarkable feat.

Non-conformity

Functioning in a traditional school classroom was difficult for Jobs, who actively resisted authority figures. He was a real troublemaker, which stemmed from boredom and his school's inability to satisfy his curiosity.

He was friends with a boy named Rick Farentino and the duo loved causing mischief. From letting snakes loose in the classroom to causing small explosions under the teacher's chair, they weren't afraid to cause a stir. They were often suspended from school and eventually separated into different classes to prevent them from causing more mischief.

The banner prank, which became part of school lore at Homestead High, got Jobs suspended again. On a big bed sheet tie-dyed with the school's green and white colours, Jobs and Wozniak painted a huge hand flipping the middle-finger salute as a farewell gesture to the departing seniors. They devised a system of ropes and pulleys so that they could dramatically lower it from the balcony, which they did as the graduating class marched past.

Irreverence

Jobs' passion for electronics began to blossom when he was only 12 years old. One day, he was building an electronic counting machine, but ran out of parts. Hewlett-Packard, the large electronics company, was located near his house and sold the parts he needed, so he simply looked up the phone number of Bill Hewlett, the co-founder of the company and gave him a call. Jobs' conversation with Bill Hewlett lasted for about 20 minutes and at the end of it, Hewlett was so impressed with the boy that not only did he give him the parts he needed, but also offered him a summer job at the company.

Intense focus

Once he'd made up his mind to do something, he would work all hours of the day and night until he got it done. Employees would sometimes get a call at 2am, or even on Christmas Day, if he had an idea he wanted to pursue. He had almost no time off and refused to give up until he had found a solution.

This intense focus on Apple was so absorbing that everything else became insignificant – social etiquette was irrelevant and trivial. It just didn't bother him if he was rude to people, nor if they were rude to him. For example, when Kenneth Ho was personally interviewed by Jobs for a Product Design position, he so disliked Jobs' direct manner and rudeness he said to Jobs at the end of the interview that there was absolutely no way he would accept the position because Jobs was, in his words, "a total arrogant jerk".[15] Jobs wasn't in the slightest bit offended, but was instead perturbed that he hadn't got his message across: that Apple was the coolest and most exciting company in the world to work for. Jobs then proceeded to do everything he could to persuade him to join. (Maybe don't try this at your next interview!)

No concern for convention

The dress code for businesses in the USA at the time was strictly suit and tie and smart appearance. However, such conventions were completely unimportant to Jobs. At Apple, staff wore whatever clothes they wanted, whilst Jobs himself cared so little that he would often show up barefoot.

Love of sameness

The clothes he felt most comfortable in were black turtlenecks (or polo neck jumpers as they're known in England), sneakers and Levi's Jeans – in fact, he hardly ever wore anything else. He would order two dozen black turtlenecks every year and owned over 100 pairs of Levi's Jeans. He also loved to listen to the same music over and over again, especially Bob Dylan.

Meticulous attention to detail

Jobs liked to get personally involved with everything to do with Apple's products – even down to things like how many screws there were in a laptop case.

He always wanted to know detailed, first-hand information about how the products were received and understood that the Apple stores provided a powerful window into user habits and needs. He therefore conducted somewhat unconventional market research of his own by surreptitiously visiting the stores. Louis Corso, who worked at the Stanford Apple Store in Palo Alto, CA, recalled Jobs' frequent visits:

> We would find him hiding behind the bushes or around the corner outside, peering inside to see what was going on. We would go, "There's Steve! Everybody play cool." We thought he was evaluating us. It was nerve-wracking.[18]

Jobs wasn't just observing the employees, he was taking in the entire experience from as many sides and angles as he could. He was staying in touch by directly observing how customers acted around his products and teasing out what they believed about his company. The design decisions made by Jobs were thus informed not only by technology trends and popular culture, but also by his direct observations and inside understanding of users' desires.

Another story of his obsessive attention to detail comes from Vic Gundotra, a Vice President at Google. One Sunday morning in 2008, he received a call from Jobs, recalling, "It was unusual for him to call me on Sunday. I wondered what was so important?"

> "So Vic", said Jobs, "we have an urgent issue, one that I need addressed right away. I've already assigned someone from my team to help you, and I hope you can fix this tomorrow," said Jobs. "I've been looking at the Google logo on the iPhone and I'm not happy with the icon. The second O in Google doesn't have the right yellow gradient. It's just wrong and I'm going to have Greg fix it tomorrow. Is that okay with you?".[19]

For the CEO of one of the largest companies in the world – the tech visionary who revolutionised personal computers, the way we listen to music and the way we think of mobile devices – to be concerned about the yellow in the second 'O' in Google tells us a lot about his extraordinary attention to detail.

Perfectionism

The constant strive for perfection did cause problems if someone in his team wanted him to compromise to get a product out on time and on budget. Jobs considered this to be a lowering of his standards – imperfection was simply not an option for him. He found adequacy to be "morally appalling". Jobs' goal for Apple was never to simply beat competitors, or even to make money, it was to make the greatest product possible, "or even a little greater". [20]

What has Steve Jobs done for us?

It's remarkable to think that a single smartphone can replace so many consumer products – the telephone, answering machine, computer, record player, CD player, MP3 player, phonebook, camera, video camera, tape recorder, radio, alarm clock, calculator, dictionary, address book, calendar, pedometer, street maps, flashlight, fax, encyclopaedia, daily newspaper, compass, metronome, outdoor thermometer, metal detector, spirit level and so many more.

Jobs' innovations have changed the lives of billions of people. He transformed the personal computer market, brought mobile computing to the general public and has truly revolutionised the way we communicate with others. The smartphone has provided education and opportunities to people worldwide - according to Statista, as of April 2021, the number of smartphone users in the world is 3.8 billion, which equates to an almighty 48.37% of the world's population.

But, for me, the most important thing he achieved was that he provided the world with a blueprint for how a modern company can

be successful by embracing diversity and employing people who
think differently.

Bill Gates (1955 -)

Many autistic people are better suited to the computer world than the social world. I, for example, am in my element when working with computers and analysing databases to extract useful information. It's almost as if my brain has been designed specifically for this task – logical thought, focus and seeing the details are exactly the required traits. Bill Gates, like me, has these same attributes, but in addition he had an all absorbing passion for computers. This special interest so totally engrossed him that, as we shall see, he didn't have a single holiday, or weekend off for over 10 years when he started Microsoft.

I have to clarify that Bill Gates has never been diagnosed as autistic and probably never will be. It's one thing to have autistic traits, but *you only get a diagnosis of autism if it has a significant, negative impact on your life*. But, I personally don't believe that autism is as black and white as simply having a diagnosis or not. Bill Gates is a perfect example of this grey area, because although he exhibits numerous autistic traits, they haven't caused him any significant problems, so he's never needed to get a diagnosis. Indeed, it's my opinion that it's *because* of his autistic traits that he has achieved everything he has done.

179

Why is he famous?

Bill Gates co-founded Microsoft, the world's largest personal computer (PC) software company. Their products have helped transform the world from an age when computers were only used by large organisations and were expensive, number crunching machines, often taking up a whole room, to one where they are now an essential everyday tool for nearly everyone.

Gates went on to become one of the most famous entrepreneurs in the world and is consistently ranked among the planet's wealthiest people. Having achieved all this, he then turned his attention to philanthropy. He now gives away most of his accumulated wealth to good causes and has set up the world's largest independent charitable foundation, with the aim of dramatically improving the quality of life for billions of people.

Childhood

Gates grew up in a supportive family environment. He and his two sisters were encouraged to strive for excellence and be competitive. Gates showed early signs of competitiveness and loved playing board games – Risk was his favourite – and he excelled at Monopoly. Funnily enough, these are my two favourites as well.

He was an avid reader and would devour anything he could lay his hands on, including a full set of encyclopaedias cover to cover aged just 11. Around the age of 12, his parents began to have concerns about him. He was doing well at school, but seemed to be bored and withdrawn at times, tending to spend time alone in his room; when his mother asked him what he was doing, he would simply shout "I'm thinking".[1] His parents decided to send him to see a psychologist, but after a few consultations they were simply advised to give Gates more leeway – to allow him to do his own thing rather than expect him to be like them.

At the age of 13, he attended Lakeside School in Seattle and it was here that Gates had his first opportunity to get into computer programming. Fortuitously, his school was one of the first to acquire a computer terminal connected over a phone line to a remote General Electric computer. Computers were extremely expensive at the time and the equipment was a new experience for everyone, the students and teachers alike. However, instead of tightly regulating who could use it and teaching the students about computers in the conventional sense, the school allowed the pupils to take the lead. This was a dream come true for Gates.

One of the other students interested in the computer was Paul Allen, who became a close friend of Gates and later went on to co-found Microsoft with him. Allen recalls the first time he met Gates:

> One day early that fall, I saw a gangly, freckle-faced eighth-grader edging his way into the crowd around the Teletype, all arms and legs and nervous energy. He had a scruffy-preppy look: pullover sweater, tan slacks, enormous saddle shoes. His blond hair went all over the place. [2]

Of the computers themselves, Allen remembers that "a lot of kids were interested at first, but they were a small group that stayed in, day and night, using the thing". [2]

Gates quickly became hooked. He started programming the GE system in BASIC and was so captivated and enthusiastic about this new interest that he was excused from maths classes to pursue it further. It was on this machine that he wrote his first computer programme, a version of noughts and crosses, which enabled users to play the game against the computer.

The GE system only allowed the school a set number of computer hours per week and when this block of computer time was exhausted, Gates and some of the other programming enthusiasts looked for time on other systems. One of these other systems later put a summer ban on the group after they were caught exploiting bugs in the operating system in order to obtain free computer time. Gates was totally absorbed by this computer programming hobby and would spend almost all his waking hours on it.

Adult Life

In 1973, he attended Harvard University where he studied law, mathematics and computer science. But, computer programming was still his primary passion and he keenly followed all the new computer developments and latest technology.

A couple of years into his degree, a company called MITS released a small computer aimed at enthusiasts: the Altair 8800. It was based on the Intel 8080 CPU, the latest computer chip at the time. Interest grew quickly after it was featured on the cover of the January issue of *Popular Electronics* and it was sold by mail order through advertisements there and in other hobbyist magazines. The Altair is widely recognized as the spark that ignited the microcomputer revolution, the first commercially successful personal computer.

Despite its popularity, programming the Altair via the front panel was a tedious and time-consuming process – requiring the toggling of the switches on the front panel – and the only output from the programs was the patterns of lights on the panel. Nevertheless, it was extremely popular, despite only being usable by dedicated enthusiasts.

Gates immediately spotted an opportunity when the Altair 8800 was released. He realised that the Intel 8080 chip was powerful enough to run the BASIC programming language, and that this would open up the market to many more customers – not just dedicated electronics geeks, but anyone who wanted to learn a computer programming language. Gates sees that moment as pivotal: "That was the revolution. That was the thing that ushered in personal computing".[3]

Gates didn't waste any time; he contacted MITS to inform them that he was working on a BASIC interpreter for the platform. The call resulted in a deal with MITS to distribute the software as Altair BASIC. This was Microsoft's first product.

Gates' vision was so clear that he didn't hesitate to drop out of Harvard University in order to take advantage of this once in a lifetime opportunity to start a software business. For most people, deliberately dropping out of Harvard would be considered crazy, but Gates was more afraid by the thought that if he didn't act straight away, somebody else might beat him to it. So, he teamed up with Paul Allen, his former school programming buddy, and formed Microsoft (a combination of 'micro-computer' and 'software'). Gates promised his parents he'd go back to college if his software writing venture was unsuccessful.

Gates' timing was perfect. Apple released their first PC only a year later and was one of the first companies to start the mass selling of personal computers with the release of the Apple II in April 1977 (the Apple I released in April 1976 was aimed at hobbyists and only sold about 200 machines). Steve Jobs and his business partner Steve Wozniak were selling a complete system comprising their own software on hardware they designed themselves – a venture which initially proved incredibly successful. The original Apple Macintosh had sown the seeds for the future of computing, but Apple had failed to understand the value of software, in particular third party software. In other words, Apple was essentially doing the same thing as IBM – selling proprietary systems that would only run their own software.

By 1980, Microsoft had grown to circa $8 million per annum turnover and it was at this point that IBM approached Microsoft for a BASIC interpreter for its upcoming personal computer, the IBM PC. IBM also needed an operating system, which Microsoft provided, but only on condition that Microsoft could licence the Operating System to other manufacturers. Gates had seen the enormous potential for separate, 'unbundled' software in the emerging PC market and thus refused to offer an exclusive licence. IBM didn't see this as an issue and therefore signed the contract (this licensing arrangement that Gates negotiated has subsequently become known as 'The deal of the century').

Every single personal computer sold by IBM from then on would run a Microsoft Operating System, as would the PCs offered by other manufacturers as they rushed to capitalise on the fast growing market with IBM compatible PCs. As IBM was the largest computer company in the world, their product quickly became the industry standard and this resulted in many new software companies forming to write application software. This made PCs more and more useful, so more were sold, and economies of scale meant that they became more affordable every year.

This had the following dramatic effects:

- The majority of computers sold worldwide would soon be running a Microsoft Operating System.
- Computing was becoming accessible to the masses with affordable prices.
- Compatibility was possible between the different suppliers and therefore, whenever a user replaced a PC, they knew their existing software would run on the new one.

Shortly after doing the deal with IBM the PC market really took off, growing from a few thousand units a year to over 50 million a year over the next decade. On the back of this, Gates became the youngest billionaire ever in the US at the age of 31 and went on to become the world's richest man from 1995 to 2008.

In another magnificent example of Gates' visionary thinking, he realised that in the same way that PC hardware had now become standardised, a standardised software suite would be attractive for the same reasons and would transform the way computers were used in the workplace. In 1988 Microsoft Office was released – a suite of applications including Word, Excel and Powerpoint. This had a major impact, because it standardised office computer work around the world; if you moved from one company to another, you knew how to use the software and if you communicated with another office, or company, most of your documents were compatible. Knowing Excel and Word became de facto standards of business. Microsoft Office was (and still is) a great success – in 2012, Softpedia reported that it was being used by over a billion people worldwide.

Another pivotal moment, not only in the history of Microsoft, but in personal computing itself, was the release of Windows 95, a graphical user interface (GUI). Largely copied from Apple's GUI, it introduced features we now take for granted, such as the Start Menu and the taskbar, which set the tone for how a computer in the internet age would work.

As if a brand new, revolutionary operating system wasn't enough, Windows 95 was followed a week later by Internet Explorer. This was the first mainstream tool that introduced the internet to the masses. Consumers began to realise that computers could be used to find a wealth of information and communicate with long-lost friends, as well as for business and entertainment. PC sales subsequently boomed – according to the Office for National Statistics, one quarter of households in Britain had a computer in 1995 and by 2001, this had doubled.

In 1998, just 23 years after its founding, Microsoft became the biggest company in the world. Windows has continually evolved, reaching a peak market usage of circa 1.5 billion Windows PCs in 2014. It's still the most used operating-system family on personal computers, with figures in April 2020 showing around 88% usage share.

Gates stepped down as chairman of Microsoft in 2014 to focus on charity work, wanting to concentrate on what he sees as the most important issues in the world today: disease eradication, renewable energy and climate change.

The Bill and Melinda Gates Foundation he set up with his wife aims to reduce health inequality around the world, in the form of eradicating AIDS, tuberculosis, polio and malaria. To date, he has given over $54 billion of support to over 135 countries. They also founded the Global Fund, which is estimated to have saved 38 million lives and vaccinated more than 690 million children since its creation.

In a bid to combat climate change, Gates launched a clean-energy investment fund in 2016, Breakthrough Energy Ventures, with the help of other famous billionaires like Jeff Bezos, Richard Branson and Jack Ma. Heading up the project himself, Gates is using the multi-billion dollar fund to invest in promising, but underfunded technologies to tackle this existential threat. As he says: "My basic optimism about climate change comes from my belief in innovation. The conditions have never been more clear for backing energy breakthroughs. It's our power to invent that makes me hopeful". [4]

Gates continues his philanthropy to this day, using his vast wealth and expertise to address the most pressing issues the world faces at present.

Autistic traits

Intense focus

According to Microsoft co-founder Paul Allen, it was Gates' exceptional focus that differentiated the two. Allen's mind would flit between many ideas and passions, but Gates was a "serial obsessor".[5] On their different approaches, he said:

> Whereas I was curious to study everything in sight, Bill would focus on one task at a time with total discipline. You could see it when he programmed. He would sit with a marker clenched in his mouth, tapping his feet and rocking; impervious to distraction. And sometimes, in the wee hours of the morning, Gates would fall asleep at the terminal. He'd be in the middle of a line of code when he'd gradually tilt forward until his nose touched the keyboard. After dozing an hour or two, he'd open his eyes, squint at the screen, blink twice, and resume precisely where he'd left off – a prodigious feat of concentration.[5]

Special interest

Gates says Microsoft was his primary focus between the ages of 20 to 30, and during this period he says he was "maniacal – not married, no kids, no weekends and didn't believe in vacations at all".[6] He didn't feel the need to have weekends, or holidays, because he found it totally absorbing and fulfilling to be hands on writing code and staying up all night long where necessary to build the business.

Neurotypicals might be horrified at this apparent lack of a social life, but an autistic person would not see this as at all weird. Gates would have been in his element spending all day discussing his special interest in programming and computers with his equally enthusiastic colleagues. So, as far as he was concerned, his social needs were being met.

I'd like to point out here that autistic people *do* enjoy socialising when it is with people who are like-minded, or share common interests. If they're like-minded then no one has to worry about making social blunders and if they share a common interest, they can spend all their time talking about their favourite hobby. What we do find difficult is to engage with people in small talk, social game playing, flowery language, or anything we're not interested in (which is therefore boring).

Persistence

Paul Allen remembers how persistent Gates was in the early days of the school computer club:

> You could tell three things about Bill Gates pretty quickly. He was really smart. He was really competitive; he wanted to show you how smart he was. And he was really, really persistent. After that first time, he kept coming back. Many times he and I would be the only ones there. [2]

Out of the box thinking

The big 'out of the box thinking' moment for Gates was his vision that software could be marketed separately from hardware. Before Microsoft, IBM dominated computer manufacturing – IBM produced everything itself, from the chips and hardware to the operating systems and software. Despite being the largest computer company in the world, IBM didn't realise the immense potential of selling software separately. Even though IBM must have had some of the best minds in the computer industry, they were all thinking along the same lines – software was simply part of 'the computer' that a customer bought. In other words, they didn't employ a diverse enough range of people and fell into the trap of surrounding themselves with people who all think alike. Conversely, thinking differently was a culture that was positively encouraged at Microsoft. Peter Neupert, a former Microsoft executive, said "The people who were rewarded most at Microsoft were the cowboys and misfits — the guys IBM would never hire".[7]

Gates' embracing of diverse ways of thinking eventually became a real life David and Goliath story when Microsoft overtook IBM as the world's largest computer company in 2015. To put this achievement in perspective, when Microsoft licensed it's first software to IBM in 1980, Microsoft had a staff of 40 and an annual turnover of $7.5 million, compared to IBM with 341,279 staff and a turnover of $26.2 billion.

Prodigious memory
In the early days at Microsoft, he knew all of his employees' car number plates and could tell at a glance who was in and who was late. An exceptionally good memory for facts and figures (often about somewhat obscure facts), is a very common autistic trait. For example, some of us can recite entire conversations from movies, while others know all the makes and models of household washing machines. I've heard of one young man who was into roller coasters; he knew all their names and where every single one of them is located in the world despite being terrified of riding them.

When I was about 10 years old, I read a *What Car* magazine, which listed the full specifications of every single car on the market at that time. I memorised every detail and would reel off the specs whenever I saw one. I didn't set out to memorise them, it's just that it was so fascinating, I found that when I'd finished reading the magazine, I had remembered everything.

Unconforming
Paul Allen's wife Rita had roasted a chicken one night when Gates was over for dinner. "Did you see that?" she said after he'd left, "He

ate his chicken with a spoon. I have never in my life seen anyone eat chicken with a spoon".[2] Paul himself recalled:

> When Bill was thinking hard about something, he paid no heed to social convention. Once, he offered Rita fashion advice – basically, to buy all your clothes in the same style and colors and save time by not having to match them. For Bill, that meant any sweater that went with tan slacks.[2]

Poor social skills

Gates can appear awkward in social situations and was known to be notoriously confrontational in meetings at Microsoft. As far as he was concerned, such confrontation was him simply telling things exactly as he saw them, with no concern for how his remarks would be received. Equally, he was completely unfazed when he himself was criticised. What other people thought of him was irrelevant – the sole object of the exercise was to find a solution to the problem being discussed. Most people would be more tactful and diplomatic, they wouldn't just say what they thought, but Gates was not to be distracted by social niceties. He was always direct, getting straight to the point. As Allen said:

> Bill liked it when someone pushed back and drilled down with him to get to the best solution. He wouldn't pull rank to end an argument. He wanted you to overcome his skepticism, and he respected those who did. Even relatively passive people learned to stand their ground and match their boss decibel for decibel.[2]

With his poor social skills and all-consuming work schedule, finding a partner and getting married was low on Gates' priority list. He met his future wife Melinda by accident one day when he was late to a Microsoft event and the only seat available was next to her. Gates reflects that "it caught me by surprise how much she engaged my

190

attention even versus all the exciting Microsoft stuff I was doing".[8] When he next saw her, in the Microsoft car park, he asked her whether she would "like to go out on Friday night in two and a half weeks time".[9] She declined, saying that he didn't sound very spontaneous and that maybe he should try calling her a few days beforehand. Gates persevered and they eventually married when he was 38.

Logical thought

Gates didn't just apply his logical approach to his computer programming – he also used it in his personal life. Prior to his marriage, he created a list comparing the pros and cons of getting married to help him make the decision. He wanted to be married, but he didn't know whether he could actually commit to it and run Microsoft at the same time. In the end, he decided to get married.

One wonders whether Gates had read about Charles Darwin doing exactly the same thing over 150 years earlier…

Messy desk

Last but not least, he reportedly had atrocious handwriting and a comically messy desk. Although these are not specifically autistic traits, they do seem to occur in a number of the characters in this book. My opinion is that this is to do with how autistic brains work logically – why devote mental energy to making your handwriting and your desk perfectly neat when your brain has other priorities?

What has Bill Gates done for us?

Nearly five decades ago, Microsoft founders Bill Gates and Paul Allen set the ambitious goal of putting a PC on every desk and in every home. That goal has been largely realised, with over two billion PCs now in use in businesses and homes around the world. By incorporating user-friendly tools such as Windows, Office and MS Paint, Microsoft succeeded in making computing (something that was remote and foreign to most people), both a personal and accessible experience.

Gates' idea that software could be sold separately led to a dynamic new industry, which promoted innovation and a dramatic escalation of the number of software products available. Prior to this, software and hardware were inseparable – if you wanted to do word processing, for example, you would have to buy a computer dedicated to the task, a 'word processor' – whereas nowadays it comes as a software package or app. We don't think twice about installing a new app on our phone; there are thousands of companies producing hundreds of thousands of apps, yet this ability to choose apps (software) that meet our specific needs and run them on any phone or computer, can be traced directly back to Bill Gates. As Steve Jobs put it, "Bill built the first software company in the industry, before anybody knew what a software company was. That was huge".[10]

As well as building the first software company, Gates shifted the value in computing to software and in doing so, Microsoft commoditised computing hardware and made computing accessible to the masses. We take our PCs for granted now, but on reflection this has to be one of the most significant events in history.

As a philanthropist, Bill Gates has made a huge contribution to society by donating billions of dollars to countries around the world to help eradicate diseases. He is also using his skills and influence to tackle the climate change crisis by providing inspiration and investment in promising new technologies with the multi-billion dollar Breakthrough Energy Ventures project.

I think it's pretty awesome that he started up a company from scratch, became the richest person in the world and then decided to give almost his entire fortune away to good causes, devoting the rest of his life to helping rid the world of disease and poverty. And along that same thoughtline, perhaps *the* single most important thing he's done is to lead the way for wealthy people to achieve respect and status by giving away most of their money for the benefit of mankind. Let's hope this trend continues.

Satoshi Tajiri (1965 -)

One of the defining characteristics of autism is having a special interest – an intense obsession with a specific topic. The diagnostic criteria for autism refer to this negatively as 'restricted interests'. It's clear to me however, that focusing on a specialist subject can enable autistic people to develop an incredible depth of knowledge such that they can even become world experts in their chosen field, as demonstrated by the achievements of the characters in this book. I see this as a very positive aspect of autism.

Most people will not have heard of Satoshi Tajiri, but I estimate that a third of the people on the planet have played the Pokémon games he invented and those that haven't will have at least heard of them. He's the perfect example of an autistic person who has focused on his strengths and turned his special interests into a spectacular career.

Pokémon was certainly one of my special interests at junior school and it provided me with a way to take part in the social world. My encyclopaedic knowledge of Pokémon gained me enormous respect from my peers – I was *the* person to come to about anything Pokémon related. I loved collecting the cards and when playing the games everything made sense, because I knew all the rules and

194

intricacies, the opposite of the normal playground environment for me.

Why is he famous?

Satoshi Tajiri is the creator of Pokémon, a game based on fictional creatures (Pocket Monsters) which players collect and train to battle each other for sport. While Tajiri himself is not a household name, the Pokémon game is a worldwide phenomenon and was the most popular video game on the Nintendo Game Boy console. Tajiri is without doubt one of the most important creative figures in the gaming world.

Pokémon has grown into a world-wide social and media phenomenon. It's even expanded into an augmented reality mobile game, Pokémon Go – one of the highest grossing and most downloaded apps – and has also been adapted into a hugely successful animated television series with over 1,000 episodes aired in 169 countries. There are Pokémon theme parks in Japan and Taiwan, themed cafés across the world and a whole host of dedicated Pokémon shops. As a result, it's now the most successful media franchise of all time, with estimated sales to date of over $100 billion (beating other successful franchises such as Star Wars, Marvel, Mickey Mouse and Harry Potter).

Childhood

Growing up in the rural area of Machida in Japan, Tajiri was a fanatical collector of insects as a child. In fact, he was so obsessed with his impressive collection that his peers nicknamed him Dr. Bug.

As an adolescent, his passion turned to arcade games. He would search out arcades run by the game makers themselves, just so that he could play the games as soon as they were released – for example in Shimokitazawa, the Taito company had its own arcade where he and other gaming enthusiasts could play the newest creations. Keen to spend as much time as possible in the arcades, he was often found skipping school just to get in more game time. Much to his parents' dismay, Tajiri failed his high school exams simply from missing so many lessons. His obsession with the arcades was obviously taking its toll on his studies and his parents were understandably concerned; they saw his game playing as a complete waste of time and were worried that he was losing his life to arcade machines.

After a great amount of persuasion, he eventually took resits of the exams that he had failed. Thanks to a focused effort, he passed his high school diploma and gained a place to study computer science and electronics (a subject that actually interested him) at the Tokyo National College of Technology.

Adult Life

Even as a young adult, Tajiri was absolutely obsessed with everything about computer games and during his studies he started writing a gaming magazine which he called *Game Freak*. The magazine was handwritten, photocopied and stapled together – making the fact that he managed to persuade a local comic book store to sell them quite the feat. This was the first time a gaming publication had ever been released in Japan and it was bursting with information about how to improve gaming skills. Tajiri used the profits from this venture to visit other arcades and play more games in order to gather new information for the next issue.

One of the early readers was Ken Sugimori, who teamed up with Tajiri and became the illustrator of the magazine. With the knowledge they gained from research for the magazine, together with their wealth of experience as gamers, they believed that they could dramatically improve the end-user gaming experience by inventing new games that would be substantially better than anything else on the market. In collaboration with a few other readers of the magazine, they studied the coding language needed and then proceeded to set up a gaming company, also called Game Freak.

Tajiri had an idea for a game with creatures based on the bugs he was fascinated by as a child. The game he envisaged, 'Pocket Monsters', comprised a set of bugs, each with a unique set of strengths. The player would build up a collection by either catching them, or trading them with other players, at which stage they could then be trained to battle with opponents' bugs. He imagined two gamers sharing information and interacting with each other using the handheld Nintendo Game Boy, which already had a cable to link two together.

Interactive gameplay of this nature was an entirely novel concept at the time and was a huge challenge to implement on the severely underpowered Game Boy. The journey to production was extremely difficult and took a total of six years. During this time, Game Freak nearly went into bankruptcy. Tajiri had to forgo a salary, rely on support from his father, and ask some employees to leave. Tenacity was certainly one of Tajiri's defining characteristics and his determination to achieve his goal eventually paid off – in 1996 the first ever Pokémon games were released.

They quickly became successful and new versions were released over the years with an ever-increasing number of Pokémon characters. Each generation of games sold millions of copies. After the video games, a Pokémon trading card game was released, which also became immensely popular with over 30 billion cards sold worldwide.

Tajiri was always looking for new and different ways to develop Pokémon. In 2016, he came up with a true game-changer with the release of Pokémon Go, with which the gamer has to go outside to effectively catch Pokémon in real life. It was an augmented reality app that transformed smartphones into real-life Pokémon detectors, using GPS data to superimpose them atop a live view of the user's surroundings. When the gamer is in the vicinity of one, they can scan the area with their device and try to catch them. This has actually been extremely beneficial to many autistic people, as it has given them an incentive to go outside, instead of playing computer games by themselves at home. Venturing out to play, they meet other people with the same interest – a perfect way for autistic people to make friends. To date, Pokémon Go has been downloaded more than a billion times.

The franchise has continued to grow, so much so that it is now a part of popular culture. References and spoofs of Pokémon have been made in popular shows such as The Simpsons and South Park. And, it's even entered the realm of science; new animals and fossils have been named after Pokémon, for example Stentorceps weedlei (a type of larva) and Aerodactylus scolopaciceps (a pterosaur fossil). There's also a protein found in the nerves of the retina called Pikachurin, inspired by Pikachu's 'lightning-fast moves and shocking electric effects'.[1]

Tajiri still works producing Pokémon products today, fulfilling his life-long ambition of wanting the Pokémon games to give children the same joy he experienced as a child collecting bugs.

Autistic Traits

Special interests

Tajiri became extremely knowledgeable about insects and this would be the main topic he would talk about to whoever would listen. I was the same – I just loved talking about my current special interest. An early example was when I went through a dinosaur phase and whenever I met anyone, I would instantly start talking non-stop about dinosaurs (when they lived, what they looked like, what they ate etc.). If anyone changed the subject, I would just carry on regardless.

After Tajiri's bug collecting phase, arcade games became his all-consuming passion. He became what Japanese called an *otaku*, a fan so obsessed that their hobbies come to crowd out virtually everything else in their lives.

Space Invaders was his favourite and he spent so much time in the arcade playing this game that an arcade boss actually gave him his own machine – he reckoned Tajiri had put so many 100-yen coins into it he must have more than paid for it! However, his love of gaming wasn't restricted to following the latest games and playing them extensively, he wanted to know everything about them. For example, he completely dismantled a Nintendo Famicom games machine and painstakingly reassembled it in order to figure out how it worked.

Obsessive collector

Tajiri amassed a large collection of bugs when he was a child, devoting all of his free time to this passion – Charles Darwin wasn't the only character in this book to be infatuated with beetles! The Pokémon game itself is essentially a collecting game, which has its roots in Tajiri's early obsession. The Pokémon slogan 'Gotta catch 'em all' came about because he understood that collecting things was driven by an impelling desire to complete the set.

Out of the box thinking

The first Pokémon game released by Tajiri was a quantum leap beyond anything else around at the time. The established games involved either defeating the opposition or completing a variety of tasks to achieve the highest score. In contrast, Pokémon was one of the first 'open world' games. Set in a fictional countryside populated by wild monsters, Pokémon compelled players to explore the fields, caves and forests of a fantasy world in search of creatures – not to kill them but to tame and train them as if they were pets.

Tajiri developed Pokémon for the Game Boy console, which already incorporated a cable to enable basic competition. He realised that this could be used to trade the bugs between players and later recalled "I imagined an insect moving back and forth along the cable - that's what inspired me".[2] This feature offered players a new, co-operative virtual experience and encouraged them to find other people in the real world rather than play in solitude.

Another example of Tajiri's innovative thinking in the development of Pokémon was the idea that it was impossible to collect all of them on your own. You *had* to interact with other people to catch them all – the games were designed such that you could never collect them all without this interactive trading. For example, you couldn't catch all 151 Pokémon with the 'Blue' game and equally there were some in the 'Red' game that you simply couldn't get in Blue.

Trading Pokémon was actively encouraged for another reason, you would get 50% more 'experience points' (XP) when using another person's Pokémon in the game. This collaborative swapping was a radical new approach to gaming.

200

It's hard to explain just how enrapturing this new way of playing games was. As one fan recalled, "Nothing was more exciting when I was a kid playing this game than meeting some other random kid in an airport and trading and battling Pokémon". [3]

Determination, perseverance and never giving up

The task of developing the advanced software required to run the Pokémon game on the relatively primitive Game Boy hardware was a huge challenge. Tajiri regularly worked 24 hour stretches and then would sleep for 12 hours, but despite this titanic effort the project proved to be too ambitious and was taking too long, so it was shut down and consequently, put on hold. Tajiri had to work on other games to raise funds before he could recommence work on his pet Pokémon project. Eventually he released a successful puzzle game called *Yoshi's Egg* and was then able to put the revenue raised into restarting the Pokémon project. Finally, after six years of hard graft, the first Pokémon games, Pokémon Red and Pokémon Green, were released for the Game Boy in Japan in 1996.

He never gave up on his goal – his willingness to go without a salary and his determination to persevere with Pokémon, despite it taking an inordinate amount of time, is the classic autistic trait of sticking at things, as seen in so many other characters in this book.

Dislike of social situations

Despite his fame Tajiri rarely makes public appearances and shuns any kind of publicity. Nintendo officials describe him as exceedingly creative, but reclusive and eccentric. At first glance it may seem curious that, despite his dislike of social interaction, he invented a game that needed to be shared with others. However, I find this idea easy to explain, because it demonstrates that he's fine interacting with like-minded people and those who share his common interests.

The game is ideally suited for autistic people because unlike typical social encounters, we can go straight in and talk about Pokémon without the small talk. If someone else has a Game Boy and is playing Pokémon, you know they will be interested by default and so a more direct approach to conversation is accepted. The enthusiasm people have with Pokémon means that we needn't worry about social etiquette. Communication is much easier when both parties know the rules of the game and you both have a common goal: to build on your collection.

What has Satoshi Tajiri done for us?

Tajiri's story is truly inspirational for autistic people as well as anyone else for that matter. He has progressed from doing poorly at school to following his passions and creating a video game that became the highest grossing media franchise of all time.

Pokémon encourages autistic kids to socialise, because actively interacting with other real-life players is an essential component of the game. It adds a whole new dimension to the idea of collecting and data acquisition, which appeals immensely to them. Autistic kids love to talk about their special interests and without this focal point, they can fail to communicate with their peers – they often only want to talk about their own obscure interests, e.g. washing machines, or train timetables. Pokémon provides a common special interest where the other person is far less likely to get bored out of their minds.

Pokémon has also encouraged regular kids to socialise with autistic kids. So, rather than being the odd one out at school (who would usually be ignored), I suddenly found myself the centre of attention when Pokémon came out, because I was the one who had all the answers and knew everything about the game.

This is one of the immensely important messages about autistic people that I'm trying to get across in this book – we can be very useful in any environment where deep knowledge and expertise are valued.

Greta Thunberg (2003 -)

All of the people I have talked about thus far are either no longer alive or have already made their most significant contributions to society. But, Greta Thunberg is different. At just 18 years of age, she's still in the process of making her great contributions to the future of this planet and is a great example of someone who has found a role in the world *because* of their autistic traits.

In my last book, *A Different Kettle of Fish* (2014), I concluded that "as the 21st century progresses, I can see the world moving into a new scientific era where the demand for autistic people's highly logical skills will increase exponentially. I feel we need to be thinking seriously about the impact we are having on the planet, which means paying more attention to what scientists are saying". Seven years later (at the time of writing), the situation is becoming ever more urgent.

The autistic way of thinking can help in situations where clear, simple and concise communication is required. In my view, an autistic person is ideally suited to address the issue of climate change – someone with the ability to be precise and straightforward, to keep to the point, keep repeating the same message and be willing to persevere. Someone who can be intensely passionate whilst remaining composed, systematic and logical in their approach.

As if by magic, Greta Thunberg, an autistic teenage girl who possesses all of the above attributes, has decided that her mission in life is to alert the world to the looming climate change disaster. She is resolute in her dedication to getting her message heard, which she is always very clear about: "Don't listen to me, listen to the scientists".[1] And, it's with this message that she points out what is plainly obvious to me – if we don't pay attention to rational, logical thinkers, we will face an existential crisis.

I think Greta is an inspiring example of somebody who has turned her autism around from being a major problem into an impressive strength. It seems to me that Greta blossomed when she discovered a purpose in life, when she realised she could *actually do something* about an issue that was disturbing her greatly: climate change. This epiphany provided her with a raison d'être as well as a role in society that was both fulfilling and rewarding. As a result, she has made a dramatic transformation from having various issues, including selective mutism, to being able to confidently address and engage with world leaders at global conferences.

Why is she famous?

Greta Thunberg is a teenage environmental activist who has inspired millions of people around the world to join climate change protests in order to force the world's leading politicians to address the pressing issue of global warming. She initiated the 'School Strike for Climate' movement on 15 March 2019, in which 1.6 million students in 112 countries took part. This led to the largest youth-led demonstration in the world in September 2019 when an estimated seven million young people in over 150 countries participated.

In May 2019, she was nominated for the Nobel Peace Prize and Time Magazine named her as one of the 100 most influential people of 2019.

Childhood

Greta was just eight years old when a teacher first exposed her and her classmates to the devastating effects of climate change by showing them a series of eye-opening documentaries. Did you know that an island of discarded plastic larger than Mexico is just floating around in the South Pacific? Neither did Greta until that particularly memorable day at school. Covering everything from the problems being caused by mankind's huge consumption of fossil fuels to the pollution caused by excessive consumerism, the fairly harrowing films were so moving that Greta cried throughout them.

But, as the lights went up and the lesson ended, life went on as normal. The next lesson would be taken by a substitute, their teacher informed them, as she was flying out to New York imminently to attend a wedding. This sparked chatter amongst the pupils about travel; how great it would be to go shopping in New York, how fantastically cheap the shopping is in Thailand and how excited one of Greta's classmates was to be heading to Vietnam for the Easter Holidays.

None of it made sense to Greta. She simply couldn't comprehend how everyone could forget about what they had just seen with the mere click of the classroom screen's power button. And, if other people had seen these documentaries, why was so little being done about it? If climate change was true, then she couldn't wrap her head around talking about anything else. How could her classmates watch a documentary showing the devastation climate change can cause and then happily chat about flying abroad, consuming tonnes of fossil fuels in the process? They were causing the problem, yet they just couldn't see the connection between themselves and the problem.

Being a rational autistic child, rather than an irrational neurotypical, the irony of such frivolous conversation following a lesson on climate change was crystal clear to Greta.

Throughout her time at school, Greta found it difficult to mix with her peers. Recalling her early childhood, she says "I didn't have one single friend except my sister and my dogs and the horses".[2] Despite this, she displayed impressive skills at school – having a photographic memory for things she was interested in being one of them. But, being different resulted in bullying and by the age of 11 she had become depressed, developed an eating disorder and stopped talking. She was later diagnosed with Asperger's syndrome, obsessive-compulsive disorder (OCD) and selective mutism.

From that life defining lesson aged eight, climate change and the future of the planet quickly became her biggest concern. Following the tough few years that led to her diagnoses, Greta came to the conclusion that "the best medicine against that concern and sadness is to do something about it, to try to make a change".[3] Her parents were first on her list when it came to convincing people to become more climate-conscious. She bombarded them with graphs, made them watch documentaries and read various books on the topic. "I made them feel so guilty", she said, and gradually, it worked.[4] Greta's mother, an international opera singer, was eventually persuaded to quit travelling by plane and her father followed suit. As part of her personal endeavors to lower her carbon footprint, Greta stopped eating meat and buying anything that wasn't absolutely necessary. As a unit, the newly 'green' family quickly began installing solar batteries, driving an electric car and growing their own vegetables on an allotment.

Adolescence
Seeing how she had changed her parents' lifestyles, Greta realised that she could potentially convince others to also change their ways.

An idea came to her when she learnt of students in Parkland, Florida, who arranged a school protest to change the gun laws in the US. Meanwhile, she could see increasing evidence that climate change was having an impact on everyone's lives – like a record heatwave in northern Europe had caused forest fires in Sweden, which obliterated large areas of land up to the Arctic. It was clear to her that she had to do something and it couldn't wait; she *had* to act immediately.

So, on 20 August 2018, aged 15, she decided not to attend school, but instead conducted her first school strike. She sat outside the Swedish Parliament with the now famous sign saying *SKOLSTREJK FOR KLIMATET* (School Strike for Climate). Whilst there, she handed out fliers with a long list of facts about global warming and explanations about why she was striking. In a bid to make an impact, she stayed there for the whole of the school day and posted photos on social media, which began to gain some attention – a couple of journalists even came to see her. Her demands were for the Swedish government to reduce carbon emissions in accordance with the Paris Agreement of 12 December 2015, in which 196 countries agreed to halt the average rise in world temperatures to 1.5°C more than pre-industrial levels.

The next day she returned for another day of striking, but this time other people joined her. She continued to strike every school day until the Swedish national elections took place three weeks later.

By then, she had attracted international coverage and she announced that she would continue to strike every Friday until Sweden aligned with the Paris Agreement. 'Fridays For Future' became her slogan and students worldwide began to copy her example and arrange school strikes for themselves. On 15 March 2019, seven months after her first individual strike, 1.6 million pupils took part in a global school strike in 2,233 places around the world, which was the biggest single day of climate protest that has ever taken place.

This tremendous show of support led to her being invited to take part in climate demonstrations throughout Europe. Her new found celebrity status as the voice of the younger generation resulted in her being asked to make high-profile public speeches at international conferences, such as the United Nations Climate Change Conference in Katowice, Poland and the World Economic Forum in Davos, Switzerland. With the whole world taken aback by her passion, it didn't take Greta long to gain audiences with world leaders, parliaments and even the Pope, who requested to meet her – a striking example of how influential she was becoming.

Her message was clear: listen to the scientists, look at the evidence and act now. She says that having Asperger's gives her a clearer perspective compared to other people. This skill enabled her to speak with a startling directness when she summed up the situation at the UN Climate Action Summit in September 2019:

> This is all wrong. I shouldn't be up here. I should be back in school on the other side of the ocean…You have stolen my dreams and my childhood with your empty words…Entire ecosystems are collapsing. We are in the beginning of a mass extinction. And all you can talk about is money and fairytales of eternal economic growth.

Leading by example, she is certainly doing her part to reduce emissions. In order to avoid the use of fossil fuels, she has stopped flying, despite needing to travel to places all over the world. In fact, when travelling to North America for the UN Summit in 2019, she decided that the most environmentally friendly way to get there was to sail, so she accepted a lift on a 40ft racing yacht. The 3,500 mile voyage took a grand total of 15 days.

Greta Thunberg is now a household name. She has gained enormous respect from people all over the world (especially from the younger generations who know that they will be the ones most affected by climate change), for her passionate and direct way of presenting the urgency of the climate change crisis. Although still a very young woman, she is filled with determination and has vowed to never give up on planet Earth; her continuing mission being to make people take action before it's too late.

Autistic traits

Focus and single-mindedness
At the time of writing, everything she currently does is focused on tackling climate change. She doesn't see the point in doing anything else if there isn't going to be a habitable planet to live on in the future. When asked how she deals with climate change deniers she simply says: "I don't".[5] She refuses to be distracted by illogical people.

Special interest
She began researching climate change after a school lesson made her aware of the crisis. It soon became an all consuming passion and has remained her 'special interest' ever since. Her life revolves around her endeavours to help avoid catastrophic damage to the planet.

She had previously said that being selectively mute meant that she only spoke when she thought it was necessary. That moment came when she discovered climate change – it was such an important and urgent issue that she was compelled to do something about it and that meant that she had to start talking.

Dogged persistence

Persuading world leaders to do more to combat climate change is such a monumental task that only an extraordinarily determined person would consider taking it on. How could a teenager possibly make any impact at all on world events and the future of the planet? Despite the enormity of the challenge, Greta is 100% committed to the task of influencing the decisions that politicians make. She says, "We can't just feel like, there's no point, let's just give up. That is not an option".[6]

Since Greta's first solo school strike in the summer of 2018, she has persevered with her demands for everyone to treat climate change as the crisis it is. Despite the Covid pandemic, and the resultant halt on all gatherings and demonstrations, Greta continued to do all she could to keep climate change in the headlines and to keep the pressure on politicians to act. She was still conducting her Friday strikes online and organising events and arranging meetings with people such as the German Chancellor Angela Merkel and Sir David Attenborough to keep up the momentum.

An eye for the truth

"I don't easily fall for lies, I can see through things".[7] In many of her speeches, Greta lambasts politician's empty words and promises. For instance, five years after the Paris Agreement of 2015, she has openly spoken about the fact that the action needed is still nowhere in sight and that politicians only focus on economics, growth and staying in power, rather than saving the planet.

Greta has travelled extensively to gather data about climate change and see what countries are actually doing to tackle the problem. One of the world's greenest major cities is Denmark's capital, Copenhagen. It's considered a role model for other cities due to the numerous sustainability initiatives in place and its aim to become carbon-neutral by 2025. Greta met the politician in charge of

Copenhagen's environmental policy who was extremely enthusiastic about their green agenda, but, upon questioning, admitted that not all emissions were included in their statistics, such as its airport. Greta saw through this and called it a "textbook example of creative accounting", where people choose which statistics they want to use to show they are making progress rather than portraying the true picture.[8] "Everyone always says we have to compromise. Everything is about creating loopholes to say they are in line with the Paris Agreement".[9]

Politicians find ways of convincing you they are doing the right thing and use clever rhetoric and statistical tricks to achieve this. For example, according to a 2019 report from the European Commission, the UK Government spends £7.2 billion a year on renewable energy. This sounds great on its own, but what they don't tell you is that they're also spending £10.5 billion a year on fossil fuel subsidies. This is complete madness!

The autistic brain doesn't have such inbuilt desire or ability to deceive, it thinks on a purely logical basis and therefore sees right through this facade.

Blunt, direct and matter-of-fact approach

Whether she is speaking to her parents, or to world leaders, Greta says what she thinks and what is important to her, without any consideration for the recipient's feelings. One morning at the breakfast table Greta said to her mother, an international opera singer, "You celebrities are basically to the environment what anti-immigrant politicians are to multicultural society". [10] To her father, upon his return from a flight to Rome, she said "You just released 2.7 tonnes of CO_2 flying there and back... that's the equivalent of the annual emissions of five people in Senegal".[11] They both agreed to stop flying from then on.

At the 2019 World Economic Forum in Davos, climate change and environmental challenges were top of the agenda and Greta was invited to speak. She arrived after a 32-hour train journey – in stark contrast to the 1,500 individual private jets that delegates arrived in. The hypocrisy of using private jets (with their huge CO_2 emissions) to attend a conference on preventing climate change is mind-boggling.

At the forum Greta spoke characteristically clearly and plainly, with brutal honesty and without any concern for what people thought about her, warning global leaders:

> I don't want you to be hopeful. I want you to panic. I want you to feel the fear I feel every day. And then I want you to act. I want you to act as you would in a crisis. I want you to act as if the house was on fire – because it is.[17]

Ability to explain complex issues simply

When addressing the politicians at the World Economic Forum, she spelt out the climate change issue as clearly as possible:

> Solving the climate crisis is the greatest most complex challenge that Homo sapiens have ever faced. The main solution, however, is so simple that even a small child can understand it. We have to stop our emissions of greenhouse gases. And either we do that, or we don't.[12]

Independent thinker

Greta is not influenced by what everyone else is doing; she's a truly independent thinker concentrating on the most important issue that the world currently faces. "I so much dislike almost anything with the world we live in when everyone tries to be the same and think the same way".[13]

Autistic minded people don't feel the need to conform and are free to think independently from the crowd. As Greta eloquently put it:

> Humans are social animals. We copy each other's behaviour, so if no one else is acting as though there's no crisis then it can't be that bad. But we who have autism for instance, we don't follow social codes, we don't copy each other's behaviour, we have our own behaviour.[14]

This is what Greta is demonstrating with her stand against climate change. She doesn't just take for granted that this is what we've always done, so 'it must be okay'. She questioned the fact that her peers had got into the 'habit' of flying to far flung places on holidays and consuming goods and energy without any thought for the consequences. Greta questions and analyses rather than just blindly 'following the herd', because that's what everyone else is doing.

Ability to see things that others miss

When Greta first saw the documentary at school showing the devastation climate change can cause, she couldn't understand why her peers then happily discussed flying abroad – which entails consuming tonnes of fossil fuels. She was able to see that they were causing the problem, yet inexplicably, they just couldn't see the connection between their actions and the problems outlined in the documentary. For Greta, the link was glaringly obvious.

Greta stresses that she did not go to school to become a climate scientist, as some have suggested, because "the science was done and only denial, ignorance and inaction remained".[15] It's interesting to reflect that a teenage girl with so-called 'problems' is able to see the truth when almost everyone else, from her peers at school to the world's leading politicians, seem to be blind.

Logical thinker

She considers it highly illogical to carry on as normal, which inevitably increases levels of CO_2 emissions, when there is indisputable evidence that by doing so, we are damaging the planet. When she addressed the Extinction Rebellion demonstration in Parliament Square, London, on 31 October 2018, she said:

> They keep saying that climate change is an existential threat and the most important issue of all. And yet they just carry on like before. If the emissions have to stop, then we must stop the emissions. To me that is black or white. There are no grey areas when it comes to survival. Either we go on as a civilisation or we don't. We have to change. [16]

Sensory sensitivities

Greta is extremely sensitive to tastes and smells and for many years ate the same food every day – dinner was always noodles, two potatoes and an avocado. She eats one thing at a time and never with any sauces, or topping.

What has Greta Thunberg done for us?

Greta has presented the issue of climate change with more clarity and urgency than anyone before her. She has inspired millions of young people to attend demonstrations, which has alerted the world's governments to the fact that they need to act now to ensure that the planet will be habitable for our children and our children's children.

Governments aren't going to do anything unless there is social unrest, or votes at stake, and the public is apathetic because they take their cues and model their behaviour according to what everyone else is doing – the 'social norm'. If no one else is alarmed about climate change, then they think that they shouldn't be. However, if they look around and see that millions of people are taking action, then they start to think that maybe they should pay attention. Greta has succeeded in getting millions of young people to actively protest, therefore she has succeeded in changing the social norm. In other words, it's now becoming 'normal' to be concerned about the climate. This surely is the most important thing she's done for us.

Her actions are producing some results and progress has been made in getting politicians to take action. For example, the UK government passed a law to become carbon neutral by 2050, two months after Greta spoke to the UK parliament, and in July 2019, German Chancellor Angela Merkel announced sweeping measures to reduce carbon emissions, acknowledging that the protests Greta ignited "drove us to act".[18]

She is also an amazing ambassador for the autistic community, helping to transform how society views autistic people and showing that they can be immensely valuable members of society. This is despite the fact that autism was a major problem during her childhood, but she has now turned it round to be a strength. She considers her condition to be an advantage "as almost everything is black or white...It makes me different, and being different is a gift, I would say. A superpower".[19] She is probably the most famous and influential autistic person alive today and is a perfect and current example of what autism is doing for us.

Afterword

One of the objectives of this book is to show that people with autistic traits have made huge contributions to society and continue to do so. Yet to truly benefit from the skills autistic people have to offer into the future, people's negative preconception of autism needs to change to a positive one where our qualities are recognised and valued. Only 22% of autistic people are in employment, yet the potential benefits of this talent pool, as previously outlined, are enormous. It's clear to me we need to get far more autistic people meaningfully employed, so we can both contribute to society and lead purposeful and fulfilling lives.

1). How do we alter these preconceptions?

The best way to change these preconceptions is to find out more about autistic people. We tend to be stereotyped – people make simplified assumptions about us based on their prior experiences or beliefs. For example, if your only experience of autism is having seen the film *Rainman*, then it's natural to assume that all autistic people are similar and thus employing such a person would be challenging. So, to learn about our diverse range of abilities and different ways of thinking, I suggest people educate themselves further. Reading this book and sharing it with as many people as possible would be a good place to start.

2). Why aren't more autistic people fruitfully employed?

The main barrier to employment for autistic people is fear of the unknown – humans have an instinctive tendency to want to mix with others like themselves. It is recognised that the interview process substantially favours candidates who are most like the interviewer and who can demonstrate good social skills and will therefore 'fit in' with the organisation. However, autistic people are different. We have a different way of socialising and a different way of thinking, so prospective employers need to be convinced that the rewards can often far exceed the small extra effort required to accommodate our differences. Which, simply put, is a combination of tolerance and understanding, along with recognition and appreciation of our abilities.

3). How do we convince prospective employers to hire autistic people?

We've evolved as social animals to live together and conform to social norms in order to get on with each other. The downside to conforming is that it stifles creativity and innovation, so we need outliers – people who think differently – to provide new ideas and question the status quo. If things stay the same, there's no change and so there physically cannot be any progress.

Organisations will move quickly to take on autistic people when they realise that embracing diversity can provide a competitive advantage. The chapter about Steve Jobs demonstrates this perfectly.

4). How do we best prepare autistic people for employment (and life)?

As I see it, the key to empowering all autistic people is to allow us to flourish by encouraging our passions and special interests. The characters in this book all had their own difficulties, but they were able to thrive because, in one way or another, they found something they were passionate about and had the opportunity to indulge in it. For example, Newton lodged with a chemist who had a laboratory; Einstein's employer allowed him to conduct his own research having completed his paid work in a few hours; Andy Warhol was given an abundance of drawing material by his mother, a skilled artist; Bill Gates had access to one of the first computer terminals in a school; Greta flourished when she was allowed to follow her passion addressing climate change and her parents supported her entirely, even sacrificing their own high-flying careers for her. Most of the people in this book did their own thing outside of the formal education system – they chose their own path in life and were supported in their choices.

Conclusion

Having read this book, I hope you are now enlightened about autistic people and are keen to embrace our differences and nuances. It should also be evident that by working together we can complement each other's skills and strengths to change the world in order to make it a better place.

And apart from that, we desperately need the autistic propensity to 'point out the obvious' to help save the planet from unsustainable human activities.

Final observation

Which neatly takes us back to the year AD33. The People's Front of Judea (a bunch of typical neurotypicals) are having yet another meeting to discuss how to overthrow the Romans. The conversation proceeds in the usual manner:

> "And, let's face it. As empires go, this is the big one, so we've got to get up off our arses and stop just talking about it!"

> "I agree. It's action that counts, not words, and we need action now."

> "You're right. We could sit around here all day talking, passing resolutions, making clever speeches. It's not going to shift one Roman soldier!"

> "So, let's just stop gabbing on about it. It's completely pointless and it's getting us nowhere!"

> "I agree. This is a complete waste of time"

At this point the news arrives that Brian has been arrested and is about to be crucified. His girlfriend implores the group to actually *do* something – to act immediately and not just sit around talking and having more meetings! Everyone agrees entirely:

> "Right! This calls for immediate discussion! .....Completely new motion ..that there be immediate action ... once the vote has been taken. You can't act another resolution till you've voted on it..." ... etc, etc. [1]

Although the film *Life of Brian* was written over 40 years ago, and set 2,000 years ago, this satirical take on how people in authority behave is as relevant today as it was then. The above dialogue sounds to me just like the current world governments' responses to Greta Thunberg's calls for immediate action to do something about climate change.

This is *exactly* why we need autistic people.

References

Introduction

Quotes:
(1) BrainyQuote.com *Albert Einstein Quotes*. Available at:
https://www.brainyquote.com/quotes/albert_einstein_148835 (accessed
15/06/2021)

Chapter 1. Isaac Newton

Quotes:
(1) O'Connor J J & Robertson E F (2000) *Isaac Newton Biography*. School
of Mathematics and Statistics, University of St Andrews, Scotland.
Available at:
https://mathshistory.st-andrews.ac.uk/Biographies/Newton/ (accessed
31/03/2021)

(2,3) Newton I (Circa 1664) *Certain philosophical questions*.
Available at:
https://en.wikipedia.org/wiki/Quaestiones_quaedam_philosophicae
(accessed 31/3/21)

(4) Newton I (15 February 1676) Letter to Robert Hooke.
Available at: https://en.wikiquote.org/wiki/Isaac_Newton (accessed
20/06/2021)

(5) Jacoby J *Sir Isaac Newton's Self-Quarantine*. Available at:
https://www.aish.com/ci/sam/Sir-Isaac-Newtons-Self-Quarantine.html
(accessed 31/05/2021)

(6) Newton I (1687) *Philosophiae naturalis principia mathematica*

(7) Henry J (2008) *Isaac Newton: Science and Religion in the Unity of His
Thought*. Available at:

https://www.pure.ed.ac.uk/ws/portalfiles/portal/9845147/HENRY_2008
_Isaac_Newton.pdf (accessed 31/05/2021)

(8) Newton I, Cohen B, Whitman A & Budenz J (2016) *The Principia: The Authoritative Translation and Guide: Mathematical Principles of Natural Philosophy*. University of California Press

Sources of information:
Britannica *Isaac Newton*. Available at:
https://www.britannica.com/biography/Isaac-Newton (accessed 20/06/2021)

Encyclopedia of World Biography *Isaac Newton Biography*. Available at:
https://www.notablebiographies.com/Mo-Ni/Newton-Issac.html
(accessed 31/05/2021)

Henry J (2011) *A Short History of Scientific Thought*. Palgrave

Jacoby J *Sir Isaac Newton's Self-Quarantine*. Available at:
https://www.aish.com/ci/sam/Sir-Isaac-Newtons-Self-Quarantine.html
(accessed 31/05/2021)

Janiak A (2019) *Newton's Philosophy*. The Stanford Encyclopedia of Philosophy (Winter 2019 Edition), Edward N Zalta (ed). Available at:
https://plato.stanford.edu/archives/win2019/entries/newton-philosophy/ (accessed 31/05/2021)

O'Connor J J & Robertson E F (2000) *Isaac Newton*. School of Mathematics and Statistics, University of St Andrews, Scotland. Available at: *https://mathshistory.st-andrews.ac.uk/Biographies/Newton/* (accessed 31/05/2021)

Westfall R (1983) *Never at Rest: A Biography of Isaac Newton*. Cambridge University Press

Wikipedia *Isaac Newton*. Available at:
https://en.wikipedia.org/wiki/Isaac_Newton (accessed 31/05/2021)

Picture:
Kneller Godfrey (1702) *Portrait of Sir Isaac Newton*. Available at:
https://commons.wikimedia.org/wiki/File:Sir_Isaac_Newton_by_Sir_Go
dfrey_Kneller,_Bt.jpg (accessed 31/05/2021)

This set of images was gathered by User:Dcoetzee from the National
Portrait Gallery, London website. All images have been confirmed as
author died before 1939 according to the official date listed by the NPG.

Chapter 2. Wolfgang Mozart

Quotes:
(1) Schroeder D (1993) *Mozart's Compositional Processes and Creative
Complexity*. Dalhousie Review Vol 73 No 2. Available at:
http://hdl.handle.net/10222/63147 (accessed 23/05/2021)

(2) Mersmann H (1998) *The Letters of Mozart*. Barnes & Noble Inc

Sources of information:
Biography (Updated 13/08/2020 original 27/04/2017) *Wolfgang Mozart
(1756–1791)*. Available at:
https://www.biography.com/musician/wolfgang-mozart (accessed
22/05/2021)

Cultbizztech By Staff (02/01/2018) *5 Things You Can Learn From The Genius
of Mozart*. Available at:
https://cultbizztech.com/5-things-you-can-learn-from-the-genius-of-
mozart/ (accessed 22/05/2021)

Deutsch O E (1965) *Mozart: A Documentary Biography*. London: Adam &
Charles Black

Gannet A (2018) *The Creative Curve*. Penguin Books

Johnson P (2013) *Mozart – A Life*. Penguin Books

Robertson C (15/12/2015) *The True Secret Behind Mozart's Genius*. Available at:
http://www.willpowered.co/learn/true-secret-mozart (accessed 22/05/2021)

Picture:
Available at:
https://commons.wikimedia.org/wiki/File:Wolfgang-amadeus-mozart_1.jpg (accessed 10/06/2021)
This is a faithful photographic reproduction of a two-dimensional, public domain work of art. The work of art itself is in the public domain for the following reason:
This work is in the public domain in its country of origin and other countries and areas where the copyright term is the author's life plus 100 years or fewer.
This work is in the public domain in the United States because it was published (or registered with the US Copyright Office) before 01 January 1926. Attribution 2.0 Generic (CC BY 2.0)

Chapter 3. Charles Darwin

Quotes:
(1, 2) Darwin F (ed) (1958) *The Autobiography of Charles Darwin and selected letters*. Dover Edition, originally published 1892. Dover Publications, Inc. Mineola, New York

(3,8,11) Darwin F (ed) (1999) (EBook #2087) *The Life and Letters of Charles Darwin, Volume 1* Project Gutenberg Ebook Produced by Sue Asscher & David Widger. Available at:
https://www.gutenberg.org/files/2087/2087-h/2087-h.htm (accessed 24/05/2021)

(4,5) Desmond A J (2021) *Charles Darwin British naturalist*. Britannica. Available at: https://www.britannica.com/biography/Charles-Darwin/Evolution-by-natural-selection-the-London-years-1836-42 (accessed 24/05/2021)

(6) Wikipedia *Young Earth creationism*. Available at: https://en.wikipedia.org/wiki/Young_Earth_creationism#:~:text=A%20 2017%20Gallup%20creationism%20survey,lowest%20level%20in%2035% 20years (accessed 25/05/2021)

(7) Van Whye J (2014) *Charles Darwin In Cambridge: The Most Joyful Years*. World Scientific

(9) Dixon B (1989)*The Science of Science. Changing the Way We Think*. Cassell

(10) Strickberger M W (2005) *Evolution*. Jones & Bartlett Learning

(12) Darwin F (2009) *The Life and Letters of Charles Darwin: Including an Autobiographical Chapter: Volume 2* Cambridge University Press

Sources of information:
Barlow N (1958) *The Autobiography of Charles Darwin*. Collins

BBC Radio 4 (08/08/2018) *In Our Time: Darwin: On the Origin of Species*. Available at: https://www.bbc.co.uk/programmes/b00gd3wy (accessed 31/05/2021)

Darwin C (1986) *The Correspondence of Charles Darwin, Volume 2: 1837-1843*. Cambridge University Press

Darwin C (1839) *Voyage of the Beagle*. Wordsworth Editions Ltd

Fitzgerald M (2005) *Autism and Creativity. Is There a Link Between Autism in Men and Exceptional Ability?* Jessica Kingsley Publishers

Gruber D B & Wallace H E (1992) *Creative People at Work*. Oxford University Press

Quammen D (2006) *The Reluctant Mr Darwin.* W W Norton

Spencer N (2020) *The Secret History of Science and Religion.* BBC Radio 4. Available at: https://www.bbc.co.uk/programmes/m000614g (accessed 31/05/2021)

The Week: Briefing (07/02/2009) *How Darwin changed the world.*

Van Wyhe J (2009) *Charles Darwin's Cambridge Life 1828-1831.* Journal of Cambridge Studies Vol 4 No 4.

Picture:

Chapter 4. Lewis Carroll

Quotes:
(1) Carroll L (1945) *Alice's Adventures in Wonderland and Through the Looking-Glass.* Originally published in 1865. Whitman Publishing

(2) Tate J, Headmaster of Richmond School, Yorks. Letter to Charles' father, Archdeacon Dodgson (17/12/1844)
Morton N C (2015) *Lewis Carroll: A Biography.* Picador

(3) Carroll L (19/12/1880) Diary entry.
Collingwood S D (2020) *The Life and Letters of Lewis Carroll.* Hotfreebooks

(4) Cohen N M (1995) *Lewis Carroll: A Biography.* Picador

(5) Wilson R (2008) *Lewis Carroll in Numberland.* Penguin UK

Sources of information:

Burgett G (18/04/2014) *A Look at The Unknown and Controversial Photography Career of Lewis Carroll.* Petapixel. Available at: https://petapixel.com/2014/04/18/look-unknown-controversial-photography-career-lewis-carroll/ (accessed 22/05/2021)

Carroll L (1994) *Alice in Wonderland: Author description.* Puffin Classics

Cohen N M (1995) *Lewis Carroll: A Biography.* Picador

Fitzgerald M (2005) *Autism and Creativity: Is there a Link between Autism in Men and Exceptional Ability?* Jessica Kingsley Publishers

Kennedy V *Riddles and Rhymes: The Logic of "Nonsense" in Alice's Adventures in Wonderland.* Whitmore Rare Books. Available at: https://www.whitmorerarebooks.com/pages/digest/4/riddles-and-rhymes-the-logic-of-nonsense-in (accessed 22/05/2021)

López V F (22/02/2000) *Carroll´s Critique on Victorian Society.* Universitat de València Press. Available at: https://www.uv.es/~fores/lcaron4.html (accessed 22/5/2021)

Popova M (16/02/2015) *Lewis Carroll on Happiness and How to Alleviate Our Discomfort with Change.* Brain Pickings. Available at: https://www.brainpickings.org/2015/02/16/lewis-carroll-happiness-change/ (accessed 22/05/2021)

Weiss Z (08/03/2009) *Logical Justice in Alice in Wonderland.* Victorian Web. Available at: http://www.victorianweb.org/authors/carroll/weiss8.html (accessed 22/5/2021)

Wilson R (21/10/2019) *The Mathematical World of C L Dodgson.* Lecture at Gresham College. Available at: https://www.youtube.com/results?search_query=Robin+Wilson%2C+Oct+21%2C+2019%2C+The+Mathematical+World+of+C+L+Dodgson%2C+Gresham+College+ (accessed 22/5/2021)

Picture:
Lewis Carroll Self Portrait. Circa 1856. Available at:
https://commons.wikimedia.org/wiki/File:Lewis_Carroll_Self_Portrait_
1856_circa.jpg (accessed 10/06/2021)
This work is in the public domain in its country of origin and other
countries and areas where the copyright term is the author's life plus
100 years or fewer.

Chapter 5. Marie Curie

Quotes:
(1) Curie M (1921) *The Discovery of Radium, Address by Madame M. Curie at
Vassar College, May 14, 1921*. Ellen S Richards Monographs No 2
(Poughkeepsie: Vassar College 1921)

(2) Cregan E (2009) *Marie Curie: Pioneering Physicist*. Compass Point
Books

(3) Curie E (1937) *Madame Curie: A Biography*. Da Capo Press

(4) Thomas H & Thomas D L (1972) *Living Adventures in Science*. Books for
Libraries

(5, 6) Goldsmith B (2005) *Obsessive Genius - The Inner World of Marie Curie*.
Atlas Books/W W Norton & Company

Sources of information:
BBC Radio 4 (26/3/2015) *In Our Time: The Curies*. Available at:
https://www.bbc.co.uk/programmes/b05n1dmt (accessed 15/02/2021)

Curie E (1937) *Madame Curie: A Biography*. Da Capo Press

Encyclopaedia of World Biography: *Marie Curie Biography*. Available at:
https://www.notablebiographies.com/Co-Da/Curie-Marie.html#ixzz6n
CKFQ57i (accessed 23/05/2021)

Goldsmith B (2005) *Obsessive Genius - The Inner World of Marie Curie.* Atlas Books/W W Norton & Company

Ledgin N (2002) *Asperger's and Self-Esteem - Insight and Hope Through Famous Role Models.* Future Horizons Inc

YouTube Biographics (22/01/2018) *Marie Curie: A Life of Sacrifice and Achievement.* Available at: https://www.youtube.com/watch?v=AFjGrVVXuvU (accessed 23/05/2021)

Wikipedia *Marie Curie.* Available at: https://en.wikipedia.org/wiki/Marie_Curie (accessed 15/02/2021)

Picture:
Portrait of Marie Curie (1903) Available at: https://commons.wikimedia.org/wiki/File:Portrait_of_Marie_Curie_(18 67_-_1934),_Polish_chemist_Wellcome_M0002559.jpg (accessed 01/06/2021)
This file is licensed under the Creative Commons Attribution 4.0 International license.

Chapter 6. Sherlock Holmes

Quotes:
(1) Wikipedia. *Arthur Conan Doyle.* Available at: https://en.wikipedia.org/wiki/Arthur_Conan_Doyle (accessed 14/06/2021)

(2) Sanders L (04/12/2009) *Hidden Clues* The New York Times Magazine. Available at: https://www.nytimes.com/2009/12/06/magazine/06diagnosis-t.html (accessed: 14/06/2021)

(3) Adams J J (2009) *The Improbable Adventures of Sherlock Holmes* Night Shade Books

(4,6,9) Doyle A C (2010) *The Sign of Four.* Penguin Books

(5,11,12,13) Doyle A C (1977) *The Complete Original Illustrated Sherlock Holmes: The Red Headed League.* Castle Books, USA

(7) Doyle A C (2001) *A Study in Scarlet.* Penguin Books

(8) Doyle A C (1977) *The Complete Original Illustrated Sherlock Holmes: The Hound of the Baskervilles.* Castle Books, USA

(10) Doyle A C (1977) *The Complete Original Illustrated Sherlock Holmes: A Scandal in Bohemia.* Castle Books, USA

Sources of information:
Conan Doyle Estate. Available at: https://conandoyleestate.com/ (accessed 14/06/2021)

Doyle A C (1977) *The Complete Original Illustrated Sherlock Holmes.* Castle Books, USA

Ellen A (25/02/2018) *Sherlock: A Cinematic Journey Through Autism.* YouTube. Available at: https://www.youtube.com/watch?v=uSdDsH8mFu4 (accessed 21/06/2021)

Freeman L S (2014) *The Autistic Detective: Sherlock Holmes and his Legacy.* Disability Studies Quarterly Vol 34 No 4 Available at: https://dsq-sds.org/article/view/3728/3791 (accessed: 14/06/2021)

Picture:
Available at: https://pixabay.com/vectors/sherlock-holmes-detective-147255/ (accessed 10/06/2021) Pixabay Licence. Free for commercial use. No attribution required.

Chapter 7. Albert Einstein

Quotes:
(1) Dietert R R & Dietert J (2013) *Science Sifting: Tools For Innovation In Science And Technology*. World Scientific

(2,5,6,9) Isaacson W (2007) *Einstein: His Life and Universe*. Simon & Schuster UK

(3) Einstein A (11 March 1952) *A Letter to Carl Seelig*. Wikiquotes. Available at:
https://en.wikiquote.org/w/index.php?search=+%22I+have+no+special+talent.+I+am+only+passionately+curious%E2%80%9D&title=Special%3ASearch&go=Go&ns0=1 (accessed 25/05/2021)

(4) Einstein A (1950) *On the Generalized Theory of Gravitation*. Wikiquotes. Available at:
https://en.wikiquote.org/wiki/Albert_Einstein#On_the_Generalized_Theory_of_Gravitation_%281950%29 (accessed 25/05/2021)

(7) Young S (11/07/2017) *Messy desks could be a sign of genius, says researchers*. The Independent. Available at:
https://www.independent.co.uk/life-style/messy-desks-genius-sign-work-environment-creative-interesting-university-minnesota-a7834786.html#r3z-addoor (accessed 25/05/2021)

(8) Crystal D *Moving Words* BBC World Service. Available at:
http://www.bbc.co.uk/worldservice/learningenglish/movingwords/quotefeature/ourexpert/alberteinstein.shtml (accessed 25/05/2021)

(10) Robinson A (2010) *Sudden Genius? The Gradual Path to Creative Breakthroughs*. Oxford University Press

(11) Berliner W (25/07/2017) *Why there's no such thing as a gifted child*. The Guardian. Available at:
https://www.theguardian.com/education/2017/jul/25/no-such-thing-as-a-gifted-child-einstein-iq (accessed 25/05/2021)

(12) White M & Gribbin J (1994) *Einstein: A Life in Science.* Dutton

(13) Waldrop M (03/02/2017) *Inside Einstein's Love Affair With 'Lina'- His Cherished Violin.* National Geographic. Available at: https://www.nationalgeographic.com/adventure/article/einstein-genius-violin-music-physics-science (accessed 25/05/2021)

(14) Brallier J (2016) *Who Was Albert Einstein?* Grosset & Dunlap

(15) Infeld L (2007) *Quest: An Autobiography.* AMS Chelsea Publishing

(16) Ziman J M (1984) *An Introduction to Science Studies. The Philosophical and Social Aspects of Science and Technology.* Cambridge University Press

Sources of information:
Bartusiak M (2005) *Einstein's Evolving Universe: Beyond the Big Bang.* National Geographic

Isaacson W (2007) *Einstein: His Life and Universe.* Simon & Schuster UK

Ledgin N (2002) *Asperger's and Self Esteem: Insight and Hope Through Famous Role Models.* Future Horizons

Musser G (2016) *Spooky action at a distance.* FSG Adult

Pais A (2005) *Subtle is the Lord: The Science and the Life of Albert Einstein.* New York: Oxford University Press

Schilling G (2017) *Ripples in Spacetime: Einstein, Gravitational Waves, and the Future of Astronomy.* Harvard UP

Stanley M (2019) *Einstein's War: How Relativity Triumphed Amid the Vicious Nationalism of World War 1.* Dutton Books

Wikipedia *Albert Einstein.* Available at: https://en.wikipedia.org/wiki/Albert_Einstein (accessed 25/05/2021)

YouTube (09/09/2017) *Inside Einstein's Mind* NOVA S42 Ep23. Available at: https://www.youtube.com/watch?v=q7Ed7tglndE (accessed 25/05/2021)

Picture:
Schmutzer F (1921) Albert Einstein during a lecture in Vienna in 1921. Available at:
https://commons.wikimedia.org/wiki/File:Einstein_1921_by_F_Schmutz er.jpg (accessed 09/06/2021)
The author died in 1928, so this work is in the public domain in its country of origin and other countries and areas where the copyright term is the author's life plus 80 years or fewer.

Chapter 8. Ludwig Wittgenstein

Quotes:
(1,2,3,6,7,8,9,10,11,12,13,14,15) Monk R (1990) *Ludwig Wittgenstein: The Duty of Genius.* Jonathan Cape Ltd.

(4) Wittgenstein L (1953) *Philosophical Investigations.* Macmillan Publishing Company

(5) Wittgenstein L (1922) *Tractatus Logico-Philosophicus.* Kegan Paul

Sources of information:
Fitzgerald M (2005) *Autism and Creativity: Is there a Link between Autism in Men and Exceptional Ability?* Jessica Kingsley Publishers

James I (2006) *Asperger's Syndrome and High Achievement: Some Very Remarkable People.* Jessica Kingsley Publishers

Monk R (1990) *Ludwig Wittgenstein: The Duty of Genius.* Jonathan Cape Ltd.

Wikipedia *Ludwig Wittgenstein.* Available at:
https://en.wikipedia.org/wiki/Ludwig_Wittgenstein (accessed 25/05/2021)

Picture:
Ludwig Wittgenstein. Av Moritz Nähr. Lisens: Falt i det fri (Public domain)
Available at: https://snl.no/Ludwig_Wittgenstein (accessed 10/06/2021)

Chapter 9. Paul Dirac

Quotes:
(1, 3, 4, 5, 6, 7, 8, 9,10,11) Farmelo G (2009) *The Strangest Man – The Hidden Life of Paul Dirac, Quantum Genius.* Faber and Faber Ltd

(2) Gunderman R (08/12/2015) *The life-changing love of one of the 20th century's greatest physicists.* The Conversation. Available at: https://theconversation.com/the-life-changing-love-of-one-of-the-20t h-centurys-greatest-physicists-51229 (accessed 09/06/2021)

Sources of information:
BBC Radio 4 (5/3/20) *In Our Time: Paul Dirac.* Available at: https://www.bbc.co.uk/programmes/m000fwop (accessed 10/03/2020)

Farmelo G (2009) *The Strangest Man – The Hidden Life of Paul Dirac, Quantum Genius.* Faber and Faber Ltd

Farmelo G (14/12/2011) *Paul Dirac and the religion of mathematical beauty* Talk presented at Perimeter Institute, Waterloo, Canada. Available at: https://www.youtube.com/watch?v=YfYon2WdR40 (accessed 28/05/2021)

Radford T (03/04/2009) *Paul Dirac: The man who conjured laws of nature from pure thought.* The Guardian. Available at: https://www.theguardian.com/science/2009/apr/02/paul-dirac-strange st-man-farmelo-quantum (accessed 28/05/2021)

Magnet Academy: *Paul Dirac.* Available at: https://nationalmaglab.org/education/magnet-academy/history-of-elec tricity-magnetism/pioneers/paul-dirac (accessed 28/05/2021)

Silberman S (2015) *Neurotribes: The Legacy of Autism and How to Think Smarter about People who Think Differently*. Allen & Unwin

Picture:
Available at:
https://commons.wikimedia.org/wiki/File:P.A.M._Dirac_at_the_blackb oard.jpg (accessed 10/06/2021)
This work is in the public domain in its country of origin and other countries and areas where the copyright term is the author's life plus 70 years or fewer.

Chapter 10. George Orwell

Quotes:
(1,6,11) Orwell G (1946) *Why I Write*. Gangrel, London. Available at: https://orwell.ru/library/essays/wiw/english/e_wiw (accessed 14/06/2021)

(2) Orwell G (1948) *Such, Such Were the Joys* - autobiographical essay. Available at: https://en.wikipedia.org/wiki/Such,_Such_Were_the_Joys (accessed 14/06/2021)

(3) Cools R (2013) *George Orwell: English Rebel*. OUP Oxford

(4) Borus A (2016) *Reading and Interpreting the Works of George Orwell*. Enslow Publishing

(5) Barnes G & Fieldman G (1972) *Breakdown and rebirth. 1914 to the present*. Little, Brown & Co

(7) Orwell G (19/10/1945) *You and the atom bomb*. Essay published in Tribune

(8) Bradford R (2020) *Orwell: A man of our time*. Bloomsbury Publishing

(9) Davison P (2011) *Orwell – A Life in Letters*. Penguin Classics

(10) Orwell G (2007) *My Country Right or Left, 1940-1943 v. 2: The Collected Essays, Journalism and Letters*. Penguin

(12) Wikipedia *George Orwell*. Available at: https://en.wikipedia.org/wiki/George_Orwell (accessed: 14/06/2021)

(13) The Orwell Foundation (2020) *George Orwell and the Future*. Available at: https://www.orwellfoundation.com/the-orwell-youth-prize/2018-youth -prize/future-society-orwell-youth-prize-2020/ (accessed: 14/06/2021)

Sources of information:
Albion Noise *George Orwell: A Life in Pictures*. BBC 4

Britannica (2021) *Cold War: international politics*. Available at: https://www.britannica.com/event/Cold-War (accessed 14/06/2021)

Cavendish D (2011) *Review: Orwell - A Life in Letters by Peter Davison*. Available at: https://orwellsociety.com/review-orwell-a-life-in-letters-by-peter-davis on/ (accessed 14/06/2021)

Colls R (2013) *George Orwell – English Rebe*l. Oxford University Press

Crick B (1992) George Orwell: *A Life*. Penguin Books

Eliot T S (13/07/1944) *Letter from T S Eliot (Faber) to George Orwell rejecting Animal Farm, 13 July 1944*. Faber & Faber Publishing. Available at: https://www.bl.uk/collection-items/letter-from-t-s-eliot-faber-to-geor ge-orwell-rejecting-animal-farm-13-july-1944# (accessed 14/06/2021)

Fitzgerald M (2005) *The Genesis of Artistic Creativity*. Jessica Kingsley Publishers

Lynskey D (19/05/2019) *Nothing but the truth: the legacy of George Orwell's Nineteen Eighty-Four.* The Guardian https://www.theguardian.com/books/2019/may/19/legacy-george-orwel l-nineteen-eighty-four (accessed 14/06/2021)

McCrum R (10/5/2009) *The masterpiece that killed George Orwell* The Observer

Shmoop *George Orwell: Childhood & Burma.* Available at: https://www.shmoop.com/study-guides/biography/george-orwell/bio/c hildhood-burma (accessed: 14/06/2021)

Tineme P *Orwell in 5 words.* BBC Radio 4

Picture:
George Orwell in BBC (1940). Available at:
https://commons.wikimedia.org/wiki/File:George-orwell-BBC.jpg
(accessed 09/06/2021)
This UK artistic or literary work, of which the author is unknown and cannot be ascertained by reasonable enquiry, is in the public domain because it is one of the following:
- A photograph, which has never previously been made available to the public (e.g. by publication or display at an exhibition) and which was taken more than 70 years ago (before 1 January 1951); or
- A photograph, which was made available to the public (e.g. by publication or display at an exhibition) more than 70 years ago (before 1 January 1951); or
- An artistic work other than a photograph (e.g. a painting), or a literary work, which was made available to the public (e.g. by publication or display at an exhibition) more than 70 years ago (before 1 January 1951).

Chapter 11. Alan Turing

Quotes:

(1,3) Hodges A (1992) *Alan Turing: The Enigma*. Vintage Publishing

(2,5,8,9) Turing S (2012) *Alan M. Turing: Centenary Edition*. Cambridge University Press

(4,6,7) Olnick M (2020) *Simply Turing*. Simply Charly

Sources of information:

BBC Radio 4 (15/10/20) *In our Time: Alan Turing*. Available at: https://www.bbc.co.uk/programmes/m000ncmw (accessed 19/04/2021)

Cooper B (17/04/2012) *Decoding the Turing Family*. The Guardian

Copeland J (19/06/2012) *Alan Turing: The codebreaker who saved 'millions of lives'*. BBC News: Technology. Available at: https://www.bbc.co.uk/news/technology-18419691 (accessed 26/05/2021)

Copeland J B (2014) *Turing: Pioneer of the Information Age*. Oxford University Press

Hodges A (1992) *Alan Turing: The Enigma*. Vintage Publishing

Hodges A *Update to Alan Turing: the Enigma*. Available at: https://www.turing.org.uk/book/update/part6.html (accessed 25/05/2021)

Lasar M (18/6/2012) *The highly productive habits of Alan Turing*. Available at: https://arstechnica.com/tech-policy/2012/06/the-seven-highly-producti ve-habits-of-alan-turing/ (accessed 25/05/2021)

Simply knowledge *Biography of Alan Turing*. Available at: simplyknowledge.com/popular/biography/alan-turing (accessed 25/05/2021)

Sykes C *The Strange Life and Death of Dr Turing*. BBC Horizon documentary

Picture:
Available at:
https://commons.wikimedia.org/wiki/File:Alan_Turing_az_1930-as_%C
3%A9vekben.jpg (accessed 09/06/2021).
This file has been identified as being free of known restrictions under copyright law, including all related and neighboring rights.

Chapter 12. Andy Warhol

Quotes:
(1,2,3) Warhol A (1975) *The Philosophy of Andy Warhol: From A to B and Back Again*. Harcourt Brace Jovanovich

(4) BBC Radio 4 (06/01/2019) *Desert Island Discs: Jeremy Deller* https://www.bbc.co.uk/sounds/search?q=Desert+Island+Discs+Jeremy+ Deller&page=1 (accessed 22/05/2021)

Sources of information:
Bockris V (1989) *Warhol*. Frederick Muller Ltd

Faerna J M (1997) *Warhol (Great Modern Masters)*. Harry N Abrams Inc

Grandin T (2009) *How does visual thinking work in the mind of a person with autism? A personal account*. Phil Trans R Soc 1437-1442

Ingram C (2014) *This is Warhol*. Laurence King Publishing

James I (2006) *Asperger's Syndrome and High Achievement – Some Very Remarkable People*. Jessica Kingsley Publishers

Laing O (2016) *The Lonely City - Adventures in the Art of Being Alone*. Canongate

Needham A (22/02/2012) *Andy Warhol's legacy lives on in the factory of fame* The Guardian. Available at: https://www.theguardian.com/artanddesign/2012/feb/22/andy-warhol-legacy-lives-on (accessed 22/05/2021)

YouTube (1966) *Andy Warhol Interview*. Available at: https://www.youtube.com/watch?v=m0KxWkXoCzo (accessed 22/05/2021)

YouTube Alux.com *15 Things You Didn't Know About Andy Warhol*. Available at: https://www.youtube.com/watch?v=rBgw3AwDZKg (accessed 22/05/2021)

YouTube The School of Life (16/10/2015) *Art/Architecture: Andy Warhol*. Available at: https://www.youtube.com/watch?v=QAJJ35DVlTs (accessed 22/05/2021)

Picture:
Available at: https://www.flickr.com/photos/krossbow/27993816878 (accessed 10/06/2021) Licence: Attribution 2.0 Generic (CC BY 2.0)

Chapter 13. Spock

Quotes:
(1) Wikipedia *Star Trek*. Available at: https://en.wikipedia.org/wiki/Star_Trek (accessed 09/06/2021)

(2) MeTV (16/01/2019) *This is the "simple logic" that convinced Leonard Nimoy to stay on as Spock on Star Trek*. Available at: https://www.metv.com/stories/this-is-the-simple-logic-that-convinced-leonard-nimoy-to-stay-on-as-spock-on-star-trek (accessed 14/06/2021)

(3) Spock *I Mudd* Star Trek Season 2 Episode 8.

Sources of information:

Irish Medical Times (09/04/2014) *Is Spock out of his Vulcan mind or just autistic?* Available at:
https://www.imt.ie/blogs/is-spock-out-of-his-vulcan-mind-or-just-auti stic-09-04-2014/ (accessed 14/06/2021)

Wikipedia *Star Trek*. Available at: https://en.wikipedia.org/wiki/Star_Trek (accessed 09/06/2021)

YouTube Foundation Interviews *Leonard Nimroy discusses Star Trek's Mr Spock*. Available at:
https://www.youtube.com/watch?v=W-Y-jrnTy5s (accessed 10/06/2021)

Picture:

Available at:
https://commons.wikimedia.org/wiki/File:Leonard_Nimoy_Spock_1967.j pg (accessed 10/06/2021)
This work is in the public domain in the United States because it was published in the United States between 1926 and 1977, inclusive, without a copyright notice.

Chapter 14. Temple Grandin

Quotes:

(1) "I am Autistic. I'm Not" A Diablogue *Dr Temple Grandin*. Available at: https://iamautisticimnot.com/dr-temple-grandin/ (accessed 10/06/2021)

(2) Grandin T (05/05/2020) *Empowering Autistic Individuals to be Successful*. Cork Autism Conference

(3) Ledgin N (2002) *Asperger's and Self-Esteem: Insight and Hope Through Famous Role Models*. Future Horizons

(4, 5) Blakely R (12/04/2014) *How we're failing children with autism. By the world's most famous autistic adult*. The Times Magazine

Sources of information:
Blakely R (12/04/2014) *How we're failing children with autism. By the world's most famous autistic adult.* The Times Magazine

Grandin T (2008) *The Way I See It. A Personal Look at Autism & Asperger's.* Future Horizons

Grandin T (2009) *How does visual thinking work in the mind of a person with autism? A personal account.* Phil Trans R Soc B 364 1437-1442

Grandin T & Johnson C (2005) *Animals in Translation - Using the Mysteries of Autism to Decode Animal Behaviour.* Bloomsbury Publishing

Grandin T & Scariano M (1986) *Emergence: Labelled Autistic.* Costello

Sacks O (2012) *An Anthropologist on Mars.* Picador

Picture:
Available at: https://www.flickr.com/photos/79383703@N08/8166666196 (accessed 10/06/2021) Licence: This image was marked with a CC BY 2.0 license.

Chapter 15. Steve Jobs

Quotes:
(1) Apple's *Think Different* advertising campaign (1997-2002). Available at: https://www.youtube.com/watch?v=5sMBhDv4sik (accessed 11/06/2021)

(2) Wikipedia *Steve Jobs.* Available at: https://en.wikipedia.org/wiki/Steve_Jobs (accessed 11/06/2021)

(3) Simply knowledge *Biography of Steve Jobs.* Available at: http://simplyknowledge.com/popular/biography/Steve-Jobs (accessed 11/06/2021)

(4) Jobs S (1990) *Bicycle of the mind* interview. Available at:

https://www.youtube.com/watch?v=KmuP8gsgWb8 (accessed 11/06/2021)

(5) Isaacson W (2015) *Steve Jobs*. Simon & Schuster

(6) Anzur T (06/10/2011) *Going to High School with Steve Jobs*. Available at: https://www.terryanzur.com/1605/going-to-high-school-with-steve-job s/ (accessed 11/06/2021)

(7) Hiskey D (2012) *Steve Jobs' first business was selling blue boxes that allowed users to get free phone service illegally*. Available at: http://www.todayifoundout.com/index.php/2012/10/steve-jobs-first-bu siness-was-selling-blue-boxes-that-allowed-users-to-get-free-phone-s ervice-illegally/ (accessed 11/06/2021)

(8) Jobs S (12/06/2005) *Commencement address at Stanford University*. Available at: https://news.stanford.edu/news/2005/june15/jobs-061505.html (accessed 11/06/2021)

(9) Dolcourt J (10/08/2016) *Apple's 40-year legacy began with this 'Eureka' moment*. Available at: https://www.cnet.com/news/steve-wozniak-on-homebrew-computer-cl ub/ (accessed 11/06/2021)

(10) Haslem K (05/03/2020) *Why is Apple called Apple?* Macworld. Available at: https://www.macworld.co.uk/feature/why-is-apple-called-apple-378350 4/ (accessed 11/06/2021)

(11) Wikipedia *John Sculley*. Available at: https://en.wikipedia.org/wiki/John_Sculley (accessed 11/06/2021)

(12) Apple Music Event 2001-The First Ever iPod Introduction. Available at: https://www.youtube.com/watch?v=kN0SVBCJqLs&t=267s (accessed 11/06/2021)

(13) Steve Jobs introduces iPhone in 2007. Available at: https://www.youtube.com/watch?v=MnrJzXM7a6o (Accessed: 11/06/2021)

(14) Cringely R (1995) Steve Jobs - The Lost Interview. Available at: https://www.youtube.com/watch?v=TRZAJY23xio (accessed 11/06/2021)

(15) Quora (2021) *An Apple employee shares – How hard did Steve Jobs work and did this change over time?* Available at: https://luxurylaunches.com/celebrities/an-apple-employee-shares-how -hard-did-steve-jobs-work-and-did-this-change-over-time.php (accessed 11/06/2021)

(16) Youtube (2010) iPhone 4 unveiled. Available at: https://www.youtube.com/watch?v=wn3OCIcE8ds (accessed 11/06/2021)

(17) PBS documentary (1996) *Triumph of the Nerds: The Rise of Accidental Empires* Available at: https://en.wikiquote.org/wiki/Steve_Jobs (accessed 11/06/2021)

(18) Kahney L (2011) *Steve Jobs Hides in bushes to Spy on Customers.* Cult of Mac. Available at: https://www.cultofmac.com/83222/steve-jobs-hides-in-bushes-to-spy-on-apple-customers/ (accessed 11/06/2021)

(19) Andri (24/05/2016) *A Story From Vic Gundotra About Steve Jobs' Legendary Attention To Detail.* Wealth Dynamics. Available at: https://wealthdynamics.geniusu.com/blog/story-vic-gundotra-steve-jo bs-legendary-attention-detail (accessed on 11/06/2021)

(20) Smith D (02/06/2019) *The Steve Jobs guide to manipulating people and getting what you want.* Business Insider. Available at:

https://www.businessinsider.com/steve-jobs-guide-to-getting-what-you-want-2016-10?r=US&IR=T (accessed 11/06/2021)

Sources of information:
Anzur T (06/10/2011) *Going to High School with Steve Jobs.* Available at: https://www.terryanzur.com/1605/going-to-high-school-with-steve-jobs/ (accessed 11/06/2021)

Bankmycell (2021) *How many smartphones are in the world?* Available at: https://www.bankmycell.com/blog/how-many-phones-are-in-the-world) (accessed 11/06/2021)

Brashares A (2001) *Steve Jobs: Thinks Different.* Millbrook Press

Britton J (2011) Hiding in the Bushes with Steve Jobs. Available at: https://zurb.com/blog/hiding-in-the-bushes-with-steve-jobs (accessed 11/06/2021)

Cringely R (1995) Steve Jobs - The Lost Interview. Available at: https://www.youtube.com/watch?v=TRZAJY23xio (accessed 11/06/2021)

Hiskey D (2012) *Steve Jobs' first business was selling blue boxes that allowed users to get free phone service illegally.* Available at: http://www.todayifoundout.com/index.php/2012/10/steve-jobs-first-business-was-selling-blue-boxes-that-allowed-users-to-get-free-phone-service-illegally/ (accessed 11/06/2021)

Ho K (2017) *How hard did Steve Jobs work?* Available at: https://beamstart.com/content/5756/How_hard_did_Steve_Jobs_work (accessed 11/06/2021)

Isaacson W (2015) *Steve Jobs.* Simon & Schuster

Jobs S (12/06/2005) *Commencement address at Stanford University.* Available at: https://news.stanford.edu/news/2005/june15/jobs-061505.html (accessed 11/06/2021)

Levy S (2020) *Steve Jobs*. Encyclopaedia Britannica. Available at: https://www.britannica.com/biography/Steve-Jobs (accessed 11/06/2021)

Okumura K (2019) *Following Steve Jobs: lessons from a college typography class*. UX Collective. Available at: https://uxdesign.cc/following-steve-jobs-lessons-from-a-college-typography-class-4f9a603bc964 (accessed 11/06/2021)

Pinker S (2019) *Enlightenment Now: The Case for Reason, Science, Humanism, and Progress*. Penguin

Reddit (2018) *11 years ago, Steve Jobs 'scrolling' on the first iPhone drew audible gasps from the crowd*. Available at: https://www.reddit.com/r/apple/comments/9kahkr/11_years_ago_steve_jobs_scrolling_on_the_first/ (accessed 11/06/2021)

Schlender B & Tetzeli R (2016) *Becoming Steve Jobs - How a Reckless Upstart Became a Visionary Leader*. Penguin Random House USA

Wikipedia *Steve Jobs*. Available at: https://en.wikipedia.org/wiki/Steve_Jobs (accessed 11/06/2021)

Youtube (2015) *Steve Jobs: Full documentary on his Entire Life*. The Entrepreneur. Available at: https://www.youtube.com/watch?v=s1dROooLyDo (accessed on 11/06/2021)

Picture:
Yohe Matthew. Steve Jobs shows off iPhone 4 at the 2010 Worldwide Developers Conference. Available at: https://commons.wikimedia.org/wiki/File:Steve_Jobs_Headshot_2010.JPG (accessed 10/06/2021). Licence: Attribution-ShareAlike 3.0 Unported (CC BY-SA 3.0)

Chapter 16. Bill Gates

Quotes:

(1) Popomaronis T (18/05/2019) *Want your kid to be like Bill Gates?* Available at:
https://www.cnbc.com/2019/05/17/how-bill-gates-parents-raised-a-suc
cessful-billionaire.html (accessed 04/06/2021)

(2) Allen P (2012). *Idea Man: A Memoir by the Cofounder of Microsoft.* Viking

(3) Wired (17/10/2018) *Bill Gates Talks About 6 Moments in His Life.* Available at:
https://www.wired.com/video/watch/bill-gates-moments (accessed 04/06/2021)

(4) Breakthrough Energy. Available at:
https://www.breakthroughenergy.org/#Breakthroughs (accessed 04/06/2021)

(5) Isaacson W (2015) *The Innovators: How a Group of Inventors, Hackers, Geniuses and Geeks Created the Digital Revolution.* Simon & Schuster UK

(6, 8) YouTube (08/12/2016) *The David Rubenstein Show: Microsoft Co-Founder Bill Gates.* Available at:
https://www.youtube.com/watch?v=KlVofyDC3Gc (accessed 04/06/2021)

(7) Heilemann J (11/01/2000) *The Truth, The Whole Truth, and Nothing but The Truth.* Wired. Available at:
https://www.wired.com/2000/11/microsoft-7/ (accessed 04/06/2021)

(9) Sellers P (16/03/2016) *Melinda Gates Goes Public (Fortune, 2008).* Available at:
https://fortune.com/2016/03/16/melinda-gates-fortune-classic/ (accessed 04/06/2021)

(10) Youtube (2013) *Steve Jobs and Bill Gates Together at D5 Conference 2007.*

Available at: https://www.youtube.com/watch?v=wvhW8cp15tk
(accessed 04/06/2021)

Sources of information:
Allen P (2012) *Idea Man: A Memoir by the Cofounder of Microsoft*. Viking

BBC Radio 4 (31 Jan 2016) *Desert Island Discs: Bill Gates*. Available at:
https://www.bbc.co.uk/programmes/p03hjzqp (accessed 04/04/2019)

Gobry P-E (2011) *Yes, Microsoft Did Change The World More Than Apple*.
Insider. Available at:
https://www.businessinsider.com/yes-microsoft-did-change-the-world
-more-than-apple-2011-9?r=US&IR=T (accessed 05/06/2021)

Isaacson W (2011) *Steve Jobs: A Biography*. Thorndike Press

Kalsi P S (2014) *How did Microsoft change the world?* Quora. Available at:
https://www.quora.com/How-did-Microsoft-change-the-world
(accessed 06/06/2021)

Mejia Z (24/05/2018) *Bill Gates learned what he needed to start Microsoft in
high school*. Available at:
https://www.cnbc.com/2018/05/24/bill-gates-got-what-he-needed-to-st
art-microsoft-in-high-school.html (accessed 04/06/2021)

Netflix (2019) *Inside Bill's Brain*.

Schlender B & Tetzeli R (2016) *Becoming Steve Jobs - How a Reckless Upstart
Became a Visionary Leader*. Penguin Random House USA

Singer E *Special Interests in Autism* Spark. Available at:
https://sparkforautism.org/discover_article/special-interests-in-autism
/ (accessed 04/06/2021)

Wikipedia *Bill Gates*. Available at:
https://en.wikipedia.org/wiki/Bill_Gates (accessed 04/06/21)

Wired (17/10/2018) *Bill Gates Talks About 6 Moments in His Life*. Available at: https://www.wired.com/video/watch/bill-gates-moments (accessed 04/06/2021)

YouTube (18/10/2016) *The David Rubenstein Show: Microsoft Co-Founder Bill Gates*. Available at: https://www.youtube.com/watch?v=KlVofyDC3Gc&list=PLi85wWwDybj zOcYNPlIi7rC9TqrEvpgBC&index=21 (accessed 04/06/2021)

YouTube (01/12/2016) *The Story of How Melinda Gates Met Bill Gates*. Available at: https://www.youtube.com/watch?v=VqsFbzTcpdc (accessed 04/06/2021)

Picture:
Bill Gates visits The Department of Energy on October 8, 2013. Available at: https://commons.wikimedia.org/wiki/File:Bill_Gates_2013.jpg (accessed 10/06/2021).
This image is a work of a United States Department of Energy (or predecessor organization) employee, taken or made as part of that person's official duties. As a work of the U.S. federal government, the image is in the public domain.

Chapter 17. Satoshi Tajiri

Quotes:
(1) Wikipedia *Pikachurin*. Available at: https://en.wikipedia.org/wiki/Pikachurin (accessed 11/06/2021)

(2) Alt M (17/08/2020) Pokémon: The Japanese game that went viral. BBC Culture. Available at: https://www.bbc.com/culture/article/20200811-pokemon-the-japanese-game-that-went-viral (accessed 11/06/2021)

(3) Reddit *Why was the original Pokemon games so popular? (Red/Blue/Green)* Available at:

https://www.reddit.com/r/truegaming/comments/6nk62q/why_was_th
e_original_pokemon_games_so_popular/?sort=top (accessed 11/06/2021)

Sources of information:
Alt M (17/08/2020) *Pokémon: The Japanese game that went viral.* BBC
Culture. Available at:
https://www.bbc.com/culture/article/20200811-pokemon-the-japanese-
game-that-went-viral (accessed 11/06/2021)

Axellian (18/06/2018) *The Man who Invented Pokémon - Satoshi Tajiri.*
YouTube. Available at:
https://www.youtube.com/watch?v=cgLShApgXW8 (accessed
10/06/2021)

Eldred-Cohen C (12/03/2017) *How Satoshi Tajiri's Autism Helped Create
Pokémon* The Art of Autism. Available at:
https://the-art-of-autism.com/how-satoshi-tajiris-autism-helped-creat
e-Pokémon/ (accessed 10/06/2021)

Madnani M (Updated: 25 Jul 2016) *A brief history of Pokémon.* Mint.
Available at:
https://www.livemint.com/Sundayapp/Z7zHxltyWtFNzcoXPZAbjI/A-br
ief-history-of-Pokmon.html (accessed 10/06/2021)

Reddit *Why was the original Pokemon games so popular? (Red/Blue/Green)*
Available at:
https://www.reddit.com/r/truegaming/comments/6nk62q/why_was_th
e_original_pokemon_games_so_popular/?sort=top (accessed
11/06/2021)

Video Game Stats (2021) *Pokemon Go Stats, Player Counts, Facts and News.*
Available at:
https://videogamesstats.com/pokemon-go-statistics-facts/ (accessed
10/06/2021)

Wikipedia *Satoshi Tajiri*. Available at:
https://en.wikipedia.org/wiki/Satoshi_Tajiri (accessed 10/06/2021)

Picture:
Photo courtesy of Game Freak's Facebook page. Available at:
https://www.facebook.com/gamefreak.official/photos/a.8294445938488
71.1073741836.804084066384924/859843314142332/?type=3&permPage=1(
accessed 10/06/2021). This file is from a shared repository and may be
used by other projects.

Chapter 18. Greta Thunberg

Quotes:
(1) Thunberg G (18/09/2021) Speech to the US Congress joint hearing of
the House Foreign Affairs Subcommittee on Europe, Eurasia, Energy,
and the Environment and the Select Committee on the Climate Crisis

(2,6,8,9,13) BBC1 (26/04/2021) *Greta Thunberg: A year to change the world*

(3) Cliff A (13/05/2019) *Meet the 16-year-old Swedish climate activist who
kickstarted a global school strike movement.* Dazed. Available at:
https://www.dazeddigital.com/politics/article/44388/1/greta-thunberg-c
limate-activist-school-strike-interview (accessed 09/06/2021)

(4) YouTube (2019) *Greta Thunberg: Eating Meat Is "Stealing Her Generation's
Future"*
PBN. Available at:
https://www.youtube.com/watch?v=krRJTj6LA8Y&t=39s (accessed
09/06/2021)

(5) Thunberg G (21/04/2019) Talk at Extinction Rebellion protest on Earth
Day

(7,19) BBC Radio 4 Today 23/04/2019 Interview with Nick Robinson

(10,11) Ernman M & B, Thunberg S & G (2020) *Our House is on Fire - Scenes of a Family and a Planet in Crisis*. Allen Lane

(12,16,17) Thunberg G (2019) *No One is Too Small to Make a Difference*. Penguin Books

(14) Kinchen R (02/01/2021) *Greta Thunberg on turning 18 and why she won't tell you off for flying*. The Sunday Times
https://www.thetimes.co.uk/article/greta-thunberg-18-flying-interview-zpf9v0x25 (accessed 10/06/2021)

(15) Thunberg G (24/11/2018) *School strike for climate - save the world by changing the rules*. TEDxStockholm. Available at:
https://www.youtube.com/watch?v=EAmmUIEsN9A (accessed 10/06/2021)

(18) The Local (19/07/2019) *Greta Thunberg 'drove us' to act on climate change, says Merkel*. Available at:
https://www.thelocal.de/20190719/merkel-says-greta-thunberg-drove-us-to-move-on-climate-change/ (accessed 10/06/2021)

Sources of information:

Thunberg G (24/11/2018) *School strike for climate - save the world by changing the rules*. TEDxStockholm. Available at:
https://www.youtube.com/watch?v=EAmmUIEsN9A (accessed 10/06/2021)

Thunberg G (2019) *No One is Too Small to Make a Difference*. Penguin Books

Ernman M & B, Thunberg S & G (2020) *Our House is on Fire - Scenes of a Family and a Planet in Crisis*. Allen Lane

Wikipedia *Greta Thunberg*. Available at:
https://en.wikipedia.org/wiki/Greta_Thunberg (accessed 10/06/2021)

Schiermeier Q (2019) *Nature's 10 - Greta Thunberg: Climate catalyst.* Nature. Available at: https://www.nature.com/immersive/d41586-019-03749-0/index.html (accessed 10/06/2021)

Carrington D (23/01/2019) *UK has biggest fossil fuel subsidies in the EU, finds commission.* The Guardian. Available at: https://www.theguardian.com/environment/2019/jan/23/uk-has-biggest -fossil-fuel-subsidies-in-the-eu-finds-commission (accessed 10/06/2021)

Picture:
Hellberg Anders (27/08/2018)
This file is licensed under the Creative Commons Attribution-Share Alike 4.0 International license. Available at: https://commons.wikimedia.org/wiki/File:Greta_Thunberg_4.jpg (accessed 09/06/21)

Afterword

Quotes:
Chapman G, Cleese J, Gilliam T, Idle E, Jones T & Palin M (1979) *Monty Python's Life of Brian.* HandMade Films

Printed in Great Britain
by Amazon

80310483R00149